Masculinities and Identities

Interpretations

This series provides clearly written and up-to-date introductions to recent theories and critical practices in the humanities and social sciences.

General Editor
Ken Ruthven (University of Melbourne)

Advisory Board
Tony Bennett (Griffith University)
Penny Boumelha (University of Adelaide)
John Frow (University of Queensland)
Sneja Gunew (University of Victoria, British Columbia)
Robert Hodge (University of Western Sydney)
Terry Threadgold (Monash University)

Already published:
Cultural Materialism, by Andrew Milner
Metafictions?, by Wenche Ommundsen
Nuclear Criticism, by Ken Ruthven
A Foucault Primer, by Alec McHoul and Wendy Grace
After Mabo, by Tim Rowse
Framing and Interpretation, by Gale MacLachlan and Ian Reid

In preparation:
Multicultural literature studies, by Sneja Gunew
Postmodern socialism, by Peter Beilharz
Discourses of science and literature, by Damien Broderick
The body in the text, by Anne Cranny-Francis
Post-colonial literature, by Anne Brewster
Feminist film theory, by Barbara Creed

Masculinities and Identities

David Buchbinder

MELBOURNE UNIVERSITY PRESS

First published 1994
Designed by Mark Davis/text-art
Typeset by text-art in 10½ point Garamond
Printed in Malaysia by
SRM Production Services Sdn Bhd for
Melbourne University Press, Carlton, Victoria 3053
U.S.A. and Canada: International Specialized Book Services Inc.,
5804 N.E. Hassalo Street, Portland, Oregon 97213-3644
United Kingdom and Europe: University College London Press,
Gower Street, London WC1E 6BT

© David Buchbinder 1994

ISSN 1039–6128

National Library of Australia Cataloguing-in-Publication data

Buchbinder, David, 1947– .
   Masculinities and identities.
   Bibliography.
   Includes index.
   ISBN 0 522 84545 2.
   1. Men. 2. Men's studies. 3. Masculinity (Psychology). 4.
   Sex role. I. Title. (Series: Interpretations).
305.31

Contents

Preface

Unless we live as hermits in a desert or as members of a community of women, all of us must every day live and deal with men, whether they are fathers, brothers, sons, friends, lovers, partners, colleagues or bosses at work. In addition, a great number of us have to *be* men each day of our lives, a task that many find to be more onerous and stressful than the cultural mythology about men and masculinity might lead one to believe. *Masculinities and Identities*, however, is not a do-it-yourself manual on how to be masculine, or, indeed, on how to be a man. Nor is it a how-to book about spotting the real men (whoever—and whatever—these may be) in our midst. Rather, it is, first, an exploration of some of the conditions and requirements imposed culturally on men and how these produce 'masculinity', that is, a set of attitudes and practices culturally deemed appropriate to men—in short, what it is to be a man. Second, it seeks to challenge a number of assumptions about men, and hence to demythologise and demystify several important aspects of masculinity, such as male stoicism or the menace apparently offered to masculine identity by male homosexuality. Third, it is intended as a contribution to the growing impetus among men to break the silence in which their emotions and feelings as well as their anxieties and hopes have traditionally been cocooned, lest by voicing these they demonstrate once and for all their vulnerability and thus their possible ineligibility as 'real' men.

The title of this book is also that of a final-year undergraduate humanities class I have taught since 1987, enrolment in which has steadily increased since the first year when some nine curious and rather apprehensive students—most of them women—showed up on the first day of class. When asked why they had decided to enrol in a unit on masculinity, some answered that they were interested to know how the topic of masculinity was going to be tackled, particularly in an era which foregrounded women's issues, women's studies and feminist theory. A few were concerned that the unit was an attempt to license men to beat their chests, look hairy and make misogynistic, crude remarks. And some thought that it was about time men examined themselves critically and found a space in which to articulate and discuss the results of that self-examination.

In subsequent years, the number of men enrolling in this unit has increased markedly, suggestive of a particular trend among young male students, at least in the area of the humanities. The earlier reluctance of male students to sign up for a class on masculinity perhaps indicated a level of anxiety about gender issues and about their own sense of (gendered) self. Many of these young men, in their late teens and early twenties, were probably undergoing the late adolescent's customary self-consciousness and insecurity, and were unready to confront critical issues concerning masculinity in general and their own in particular. Many, to judge from the expressions and gestures of impatience from male students in this and other classes when the topic of feminism was raised, evidently felt threatened and beleaguered by feminism and by fledgling feminists who were their fellow students and who no doubt also began to appear more and more in the social circles these young men frequented; and so they were possibly unwilling to commit themselves to a course which would require them to confront problems of gender and social inequity directly. Gender issues, after all, have usually been viewed by men as women's work, and indeed men have usually left women to navigate those perilous seas on behalf of *both* sexes.

That more male students are now developing an interest in men's studies suggests that the climate is changing, at least among the student population with which I am familiar. These young men are willing to discuss their sexuality (or, rather, sexualities), their social fears and preoccupations, the baffling and often contradictory requirements made of them by the current cultural construction of masculinity, and the like; and they do so with both the women in the class and the other men—an important point, for while women often act as confidantes to men, the latter are generally reluctant to trust their confidences to others of their own sex.

Nor is the topic of male homosexuality as taboo as it once was. Whereas the female students always seemed ready to discuss this subject, some of the males used to express reservations, repugnance or simply embarrassment regarding male homosexuality. Now the men will explore some of the issues surrounding male homosexuality, if not with eagerness, then at least with interest, since what they discover impinges on their own sense of self, whether or not they are themselves gay.

At the end of this unit I have customarily asked the students to think about what they have discovered about men and masculinity during the course of the semester, and to share with the group any of their observations. Interestingly, their responses have fallen into a strong pattern divided by the line of gender. Although such a unit as this necessarily focuses on men and thus in a special sense runs the danger of repeating the marginalisation of women and women's issues by the broader culture, nonetheless a number of the women have brought those issues to the class discussions and have thereby broadened the range of these. Some of these students, however, have remarked that they had not before been fully aware of the sorts of pressures faced by men each day of their lives, pressures emanating from other men and from the dominant, patriarchal model of masculinity; nor had they realised the enormous and crippling efforts made by most men to efface their anxieties and emotions in order to present a reasonable, impassive face to the world. In ironic contrast, many of the men have responded to my question by saying that though *they* had always known and felt these things (and others discussed during the course of the semester), they had not realised that *other* men also knew and felt them—an illuminating as well as saddening comment about men's sense of isolation, and the emotional confusion and impoverishment forced on men by their need to keep up an impervious, stoic façade. Many, too, were surprised at the importance of both feminism and gay political activism to the development of a theorisation of masculinity (a topic discussed further in chapter one).

Masculinities and Identities does not attempt to replicate all the material in the unit, but rather offers a sketch of some of the issues confronting both men and students of masculinity. Many points important to a discussion of masculinity have necessarily been omitted as a consequence, and therefore some readers may feel dissatisfied that the book does not deal with certain issues. For instance, the question of work and its place in the dynamic of masculinity is touched on only briefly; issues to do with the family and with fathering are not directly addressed; nor have I paid as much attention as the matter deserves to differences generated by social class. Some readers may feel, too, that the masculinities described and commented on in the book do not accurately match their own experience and knowledge.

A further signal omission is the matter of ethnic or racial difference in the construction of masculinity, the chief object of attention here being the white, Anglo (mostly middle-class) man. This model of masculinity is the one held up persistently and powerfully in most English-speaking countries, in the distribution of social and political power as well as in the media, particularly in advertising. It is, therefore, likely to be familiar to others of whatever ethnic or racial background, and, precisely because of its pervasiveness and its power, deserves to be examined carefully and critically. How masculinity may be constructed according to ideologies of race or ethnicity and how masculinity is constructed in other cultures are important issues, but they are not dealt with here, though I have included some entries in the bibliography which do address these topics. For instance, the essays by Kobena Mercer and Isaac Julien, 'Race, Sexual Politics and Black Masculinity: A Dossier' (Chapman and Rutherford, 1988:97–164), and Robert Staples, 'Masculinity and Race: The Dual Dilemma of Black Men' (Kimmel and Messner, 1989:73–83) are by black men dealing with gender and sexual issues faced by men of colour in a predominantly white society. Paul Hoch's *White Hero, Black Beast: Racism, Sexism and the Mask of Masculinity* (1979) explores, from the position of a white man, the attitudes of white, western society toward men of colour, while others—Nicholas Bornoff's *Pink Samurai: The Pur-suit and Politics of Sex in Japan* (1991), for example, or Bret Hinsch's *Passions of the Cut Sleeve: The Male Homosexual Tradition in China* (1990)—contain accounts of male sexuality in other cultures, but are written by men of race or ethnicity different from those examined and so should be read bearing in mind that their observations are likely to be filtered through a particular ethnic, cultural and social lens. A particularly interesting account of western male sexuality is offered by David Henry Hwang, a Chinese American, in his play *M. Butterfly* (1988) and in the Afterword which accompanies the printed version. Hwang's own dual eth-nicity positions him to make telling comments about the attitudes of western men regarding, for instance, the sexual availability and submissiveness of Asian women, part of what Edward Said de-scribes as the 'Orientalism' of the west (1978).

The reader already familiar with theories of gender might expect the present book to engage some of the debate currently problematising certain ideas or terms, for instance, the relation of sex to gender, and of both of these to the notion of identity, as discussed by Judith Butler in her book *Gender Trouble: Feminism and the Subversion of Identity*. Butler deconstructs the notion, advanced by Gayle Rubin in 'The Traffic in Women: Notes on the "Political Economy" of Sex' (1975), of a sex/gender system, arguing instead that the relation of sex (male or female) to gender (masculine or feminine) should not be conceived as analogous to that of nature to culture, and that the very notion of sex, which appears to be the absolute basis of any discussion of gender, is itself dependent upon a silent, prior set of assumptions about gender (1990:6–7). None the less, Rubin's notion of a sex/gender system, though vulnerable to the sort of interrogation which Butler applies, remains a useful way of thinking through a number of gender issues. (It is worth noting, incidentally, that Butler's argument itself comes in the end to depend implicitly upon a similar binary distinction between sex and gender.) In the interest of clarity, therefore, I have not attempted to represent the various 'hot spots' in current discussions about gender theory, though, as is the case with the topic of race and gender, many of the entries in the suggestions for further reading do address such issues.

More scholarship in the area of masculinity still needs to be done, for example, on the history of the masculine in different periods and in different cultures; the history of men's studies and the theorisation of masculinity; and a survey of the kinds of theories—drawn from disciplines like sociology, psychology, cultural studies and so on—employed in examinations of masculinity. These are important tasks; but they are outside the scope of the present guide to the study of masculinity. To other studies and to other scholars, then, I leave these issues. Instead, I have set myself the task of sketching out some important areas of concern to such study, highlighting issues intended to provoke the reader into thinking about her or his assumptions about masculinity, male sexuality and the like, and to encourage her or him to explore the field further.

In the chapters which follow, the theorisation of masculinity is combined with readings of various kinds of cultural 'text', ranging across several genres and drawn from the early years of the twentieth century to the present, both to illustrate theoretical points and to further the theorisation itself. The book sets up some of the central issues and terms in Chapter 1 and develops them further in Chapter 2 in a reading of an operatic text, Bartók's *Duke Bluebeard's Castle*, as an allegory of the structure of the masculine. That is, the reading explores the text from the perspective of what it has to say about men. Chapter 3, illustrating its points from the movies *Tootsie* and *Some Like It Hot*, considers marginal masculinities, specifically transvestism and homosexuality, exploring how these not only contravene the dictates of dominant notions about masculinity but also raise confronting questions about that dominance. Inevitably, the discussion also engages the issue of homophobia implied in the culture's model of masculinity. The final chapter, teasing out some of the implications of a lawsuit concerning the publication of a photograph of a nude Rugby League player, looks at phallocentrism, a key term and concept in much feminist theory; and it concludes by imagining a possible masculinity of the future.

If the range of texts chosen strikes the reader as eclectic (and an opera an especially unlikely choice), then an implicit point has been made: gender issues are not the province only, say, of literary texts or of literary criticism or of movies made within the last decade, when film-makers have responded to the demands made elsewhere in the culture by women. The texts discussed here have therefore been drawn from both so-called 'high' and popular culture in order to demonstrate the pervasiveness of certain structures and dynamics of masculinity. The readings are intended to model ways of (re-)reading cultural materials from the perspective of gender and, specifically, of masculinity, but are not offered as fully argued, complete analyses of the respective texts.

Objections to the inclusion of an operatic text may be answered by pointing out that not even those texts deemed 'high-cultural' are exempt from issues of gender and masculinity. (The operas of Verdi, for instance, seem to centre almost obsessively on the consequences—for men as well as women—of actions initiated by dominant male figures of authority, whether dukes or fathers, while the narrative line of Wagner's operatic cycle, *The Ring of the Nibelungs*, is propelled by the decisions and actions of autocratic, often literally patriarchal figures, commencing with Alberich's seizure of the Rhinegold and Wotan's decision to build Valhalla.) Attention in the discussion of *Duke Bluebeard's Castle* is drawn to the narrative, not the music, as being more immediately accessible to the reader, and providing a model for other kinds of narrative. Even though the analyses of the selected texts are not exhaustive, I hope they offer ways of (re-)reading social issues and texts so as to expose often-hidden discourses of gender.

A brief word on terminology should be said at this point. Writing a book about men poses a problem for a male author: should he refer to men as 'they' or 'we'? 'They' implies a distancing of the author from his topic, as though he himself were above the issues and complexities about which he writes, observing and speaking from an Olympian vantage-point. 'We', by contrast, clearly marks the author's identification with both his sex and his topic, but in that very identification creates a cosiness which, on the one hand, might invite a confessional and perhaps, for some readers, embarrassingly intimate tone (by no means unusual in some of the literature on and by men); and/or, on the other, exclude the female reader, which is not at all the intention here. I have, therefore, gone for the 'they' option, but wish to signal that I do not thereby implicitly claim, as though under some kind of divine dispensation, freedom from the structures and dynamics affecting other men in the culture.

Where I have employed a term commonly used in gender theory,

I have either glossed it, or used it in such a way as—I trust—to make its meaning clear. However, in much of the literature on gender, as also on general theory and on cultural studies (all relevant to the theme of this book), the terms 'society' and 'culture' (and their derivatives, such as 'social', 'cultural') are often used almost interchangeably, blurring any distinct meaning they once had. I employ 'society' and 'social' where the reader's attention is directed to structures like class or to specific and actual behaviours, and 'culture' and 'cultural' where I wish to foreground a more nebulous aggregation of attitudes and ways of thinking or behaving, as well as myth (in the semiotic, Barthesian sense) and ideology. Though these are implicit in social structures and behaviours, they are often less tangible.

In addition to the term 'discourse', which is current in much writing on gender (it is defined and explained in Chapter 2), I have also invoked the idea of a dominant model of masculinity. However, lest the reader mistake the term to suggest narrowly that there is a unitary, totalising model, I wish to bring to her or his attention a definition of 'model' offered by Itamar Even-Zohar which identifies the model as built of three parts: the possible and available elements, the rules for combination of these, and the possible combinations (1990:41). This notion of model is perhaps best understood by analogy with a motor vehicle: the latter may have, in addition to a particular design, a variety of 'optional extras', such as the kind and colour of the upholstery fabric, a sunroof, a radio, a tapedeck and so on. In addition, the vehicle owner may (re-)decorate both the interior and the exterior of his car in order to personalise it. Some types of car, moreover, may be used for different purposes: a station wagon, for example, may be used to transport heavy equipment or to ferry the kids around from place to place. Yet the *model* of car remains the same. If we apply this to the notion of masculinity, we may say that the dominant model has access to a variety of elements, ranging through physical types, ethnicities, classes, sexualities, occupations and so on, which allows for a very great range of types of men. However, only some combinations of these will be admitted by the culture at any given historical moment, foregrounded and privileged as 'truly' masculine. The model, then, is potentially very flexible, but its possibilities are generally limited by cultural dictates and by historical circumstances. Those limited possibilities function as the dominant model of masculinity.

My thanks are due to Ken Ruthven, the general editor of the Interpretations series, and to John Iremonger, of Melbourne University Press, for their invitation to me to write this volume for the series and for their assistance and patience. I wish also to thank Boosey and Hawkes (Australia) Pty Ltd for permission to quote from Chester Kallman's translation of Bartók's *Duke Bluebeard's Castle*. I am also indebted to many others, not the least of these the students who have enrolled in my class on masculinity, have questioned and challenged me, and helped me to shape my thinking about the topic. I want, too, to acknowledge the help and assistance of friends and colleagues who have asked me important questions about my work in men's studies, offered support and generously consented to read and criticise parts or all of the several drafts through which the book evolved. By name, these noble souls are Ron Blaber, Robert Curry, John Fielder, Jodi Kerslake, Louise Hulton, Jene Lloyd Myles, Ann McGuire, Margaret Macintyre, Brian Moon, Sarah Schladow and Steve Singer. I particularly wish to thank Brian Dibble and Barbara Milech for their keen interest in my work in the area of men's studies and for their painstaking reading of the manuscript, together with their invaluable help in revising it. May the Good Gender-Angel visit all these people with benisons aplenty!

Finally, I hope that the chapters that follow will leave the reader with that same strange combination of surprise and familiarity which my students expressed, and which is often also the effect of looking at ourselves in a mirror.

1

Masculinities and Identities

Masculinit*ies*? A *plurality* of masculinity? Twenty years ago such an idea would have been, to say the least, unusual. And twenty years before that, probably unthinkable. Masculinity has traditionally been seen as self-evident, natural, universal; above all as unitary and whole, not multiple or divided. What has happened, then, in recent decades to produce an ever-rising flood of journal articles, books, radio programmes and television series dedicated to exploring masculinity as though it were a problem, or at least subject to question? How is it that the plural of 'masculinity' has become almost an orthodoxy of those presently researching, writing and teaching in the area of what we may call men's studies?

In the last few years a number of writers and scholars, as well as the media, have announced that masculinity is in crisis and that men are now less certain of themselves than ever before. Some reasons for this are no doubt fairly self-evident. For example, the higher profile, especially since the advent of HIV/AIDS, of male homosexuals and of bisexuals not only in the media but also in day-to-day interaction and conversation has helped to fragment the notion of masculinity. It is no longer as easy as it once was to define heterosexual men as masculine, and homosexual ones as, if not feminine or effeminate, then at least non-masculine. Machismo, that is, aggressive maleness or hypermasculinity, is no longer the province only of the heterosexual: many gay men in the 1980s adopted the macho look, spending hours each day in gyms to achieve the perfect, muscular body that would cause them to appear no different from the most heterosexual of their brethren. In addition, the public disclosure of their homosexuality by many gay men of various temperaments and appearance has tended to undermine the popular stereotype of the limp-wristed and lisping male homosexual.

The rise of the New Age Man has also blurred older, more traditional distinctions between what is considered manly or masculine and what is therefore unmanly, unmasculine. This variety of man is supposedly gentler and less aggressive than Old Age Man, more in harmony with the earth and with nature, less convinced of the authority and rightness of traditional male logic, and more amenable to alternative ways of thinking. He attempts to get in touch with his feelings, and is willing to make himself vulnerable, emotionally, to others. Such a man is very different, obviously, from the aggressive, self-contained, independent man whom our culture tends traditionally to associate with the idea of masculinity.

So we may conclude that the older model of masculinity more and more is being perceived as narrow and as creating simply the illusion that 'masculinity' is unitary and whole. Though masculinity and femininity are often popularly spoken of as if they were innate qualities of men and women, it would be truer to say that the masculine is what men in their immense variety *do*, just as the feminine is what women *do*, rather than what men and women *are* (cf. Morgan, 1992:47). If it were a fact that masculinity is written genetically into male bodies, it would not, surely, be necessary for parents to tell tearful little boys that 'Big boys don't cry'. Nor would it be necessary, when boys are somewhat older, to require them to perform difficult, often physically and emotionally painful tasks in order that these 'make men' of them. Indeed, the idea that particular tasks would 'make men' of boys suggests that the requisite behaviour might not come unaided to the young males in question. Put otherwise, behaviour characterised as masculine or feminine, in the first place, is *learned*; and, in the second, it is what we *do* in order to be acknowledged as men/masculine or women/feminine. And this may in turn govern how we feel and react as men or women.

Such gendered behaviour is founded on the primary sexual differences which divide us, male from female. However, it is not sexual difference alone which determines how we behave, how we feel and how we think—as the example above suggests, little boys can cry as well or as much as little girls. But there are codes for each sex, codes which for the most part evolved at some distant point in the culture's history. These are renewed and from time to time modified with each generation, and powerfully influence how we think and function socially and personally. 'Male' and 'female', then, are *biological* terms: they point to anatomical, primarily genital difference. 'Man' and 'woman', however, are *gendered* terms, and signify social, that is, behavioural and experiential, difference. They are categories with certain coded behaviours which we as young males or females must learn in order to become men or women. Masculinity and femininity thus are not *inherent* characteristics.

This is not to say that sexual difference is itself somehow neutral. As Judith Butler observes, the very notion of a sexual differentiation already presupposes gender difference (1990:6–7 ff.). The relation of sex to gender is thus *binary* or systemic in that each term depends on the existence of the other, the meaning of the system and its components being determined by the culture. The body, then, is not a sort of blank space on which sexual and thence gender identity gradually become visible. After all, one of the first things a parent wants to know about a newborn child, and one of the first things the midwife, doctor or nurse tells the parent, is its sex. Thus we might say that the sexing of the infant's body already starts to map on to that body both a history and a future defined and dictated by gender expectations: if the infant is a boy, his anticipated future as a male is already conceived in terms of the past experience of the men/boys around him. Buying the infant blue baby clothes or, later, toy trucks, for instance, is both to confirm those expectations and to set in motion the process whereby it is anticipated they will be met.

As gender concepts or models for people in the culture, however, masculinity and femininity are not unchanging and transhistorical but depend rather on current cultural, political, social and historical determinants. None the less, 'masculine' and 'feminine' are often used as though their meanings were immutable and permanent in an effort to codify, contain and render fixed a wide spectrum of the continually changing attitudes and practices of real men and women. These terms and their associated concepts attempt to normalise and control through ideology what is by its very nature various and not easily amenable to uniformity, namely, humanity itself. But then our culture has not historically been one that has overtly encouraged diversity: the account of religious wars and controversies alone in the western world testifies to this. And so it is with masculinity and femininity: there are norms, standards or models to which men and women in the culture are expected to conform if they wish to interact appropriately and acceptably with others. We might note that these norms are often persuasively supervised, patrolled and enforced, for instance by religion through various doctrines (and dogmas), together with their consequent encouragements and strictures, and/or by society, through permissions or prohibitions articulated by legislation and the machinery of the law (juridical procedure, for example).

It is to the differences between the biological and the social that the idea of what Gayle Rubin (1975:159) has called a *sex/gender system* refers. Such a system is *semiotic* in nature in that it assigns meaning to sexual difference and to the differential behaviours of men and women. (Semiotics is the study of signs and sign-systems, and how these are produced and recognised in a given culture at a given historical moment.) These meanings may appear, to the members of a society, natural and hence inevitable and universal. However, meaning is always mediated through and influenced by cultural and historical circumstances. What we in western cultures toward the end of the twentieth century think it is to be a man must be very different from what, say, a traditional people living along the Amazon River in Brazil think, or what our ancestors in the eighth century might have thought.

We may identify theories of gender as generally falling into one of two categories. The first is *essentialism*: this asserts that masculine or feminine traits are innate (essences) in the individual. This idea underlies common, popular notions of gender. The exhortation to a male, 'Be a man!', is thus understood not so much to mean, 'Learn what it is to be a man in our culture and adopt that set of behaviours henceforth', but rather, 'There is within you a set of masculine traits that, once recognised and freed, will enable you to be a man'.

Essentialist theories of gender, however, are not limited to the popular. They also appear in the guise of scientific—including psychological and sociological—theory. For instance, hypotheses that modern man has adapted hunting instincts inherited from primitive human existence in an archaic world, so that the city becomes the modern equivalent of the early savannahs on which our ancestors may once have roamed in search of food for the tribe, are based on the notions that such instincts are essential, that is, innate, in men. Likewise, research to determine the chemical or biological 'cause' of homosexuality presupposes that it is a failure or distortion of 'the normal', namely, essential heterosexuality.

In this category may be included the claim of Dr Simon LeVay of the Salk Institute to have discovered that a certain part of the hypothalamus is smaller in women and gay men than in straight men. Setting aside the truth or accuracy of this claim, which, one would imagine, depends on whether the number of instances is convincingly large, whether the fact that many of the subjects had been victims of HIV/AIDS may have contributed to the condition of the hypothalamus, and whether, correspondingly, the relevant part of the hypothalamus in lesbian women is the same size as that in straight men (and if not, why not)—a logical implication of the doctor's announcement—certain questions remain. First, how is this information to be treated, and will gay men continue to be classified as abnormal (and hence further marginalised and perse-cuted) on the basis of size in this particular gland? There is also the matter of whether attempts may be made to 'correct' the possible homosexuality of the unborn male child in the womb by detecting the size of the foetal hypothalamus and the subsequent administer-ing of chemicals such as hormones. Second, there is the matter of whether hypothalamus size is a decisive factor in determining the orientation of an individual, and whether the size of the gland produces the orientation or is regulated by that orientation. There are, therefore, two issues here: the scientific determination of the 'cause' of something deemed to be unusual, eccentric or abnormal; and what kind of meaning this will have in the culture and what kind of effect on the lives of individuals defined as falling into that category. (See Barinaga, 1991; LeVay, 1991.) Ironically, LeVay's findings, viewed from another position, may in fact demonstrate that it is the heterosexual male's hypothalamus which is abnormal, if women and homosexual men turn out to be the statistical majority. Even so, we may suspect that we will be unlikely to hear calls to have the excess growth in their hypothalamus gland removed from the brains of heterosexual men.[1]

There are two principal difficulties with essentialist theories of gender. The first is that they effectively deny the possibility of change and discourage attempts at it. Evolutionary development becomes conceived as merely the temporary adaptation of intrinsic, immutable characteristics to the immediate conditions of living. If this is really the case, then such projects as attempts to bring about equality between the sexes or to reduce violent behaviour (perpetrated mostly by men) in society are ultimately futile. Essentialism creates a social division between the sexes that is much sharper and more obstructive than the anatomical division created by genital difference. Men are defined by essentialist gender theory as so different from women that they become almost a different species: territorial, aggressive, violent and so on. The most we could hope for, then, is a coercive holding operation, enabled by legislation, to protect the weaker and more vulnerable members of society from such predatory behaviour.

The second difficulty with essentialism is that, as we have seen from the example of LeVay's hypothesis, it invites dangerous notions of 'curing' deviance from some set of characteristics thought of as essential and hence normal. Homosexuality is an obvious candidate for such treatment, whether as 'cure' or as behaviour modification. Yet homosexuality is deviant or abnormal only where heterosexuality is defined as the only real option for the normal male. Not all cultures have seen male sexuality that way, whether in antiquity (ancient Greece, for instance) or in the present century (parts of Africa and Melanesia, for example; see Rubin, 1993; Greenberg, 1988). Other sorts of people have also been subjected to 'cures' or modifications, for instance, the mentally handicapped and neurotics. The logical extreme of this approach is the doctrine of eugenics, which seeks to breed selectively for a better human race and which developed toward the end of the nineteenth century in Europe as the result of the application of Charles Darwin's theory of natural selection and adaptation to social issues. It found its most extreme expression in the Nazi programme to eliminate the racial 'impurity' represented by Jews, gypsies, homosexuals, and other 'non-Aryans' or deviants.

The second category of gender theory is *constructionism* (sometimes also called 'constructivism'). This type of theory proposes that gender is not innate but rather learned or constructed; and that gender constructions and behaviours are the result of intersecting historical, cultural and social factors at particular moments in a culture's life. It thus allows for change in such constructions and behaviours, since it sees these as dependent on changing circumstances. From the constructionist perspective, changing *practices*, such as, for instance, eliminating sexist language from both official and unofficial communications, will also cause *attitudes* to change. Moreover, though it also permits different constructions and behaviours to be considered as alternatives, rather than as abnormalities, constructionist theory also recognises that in any culture at a given moment certain gender constructions as behaviours are dominant and hence considered norm*ative* (as opposed to norm*al*) for that culture. ('Normal' indicates the usual or common state of things, whereas 'normative' proposes that people and practices be regularised and homogenised in order to conform to a pre-ordained belief about how things ought to be.) Constructionist theory would thus argue that male homosexuality is not in itself abnormal but may be considered and thence treated so in a specific culture. By the same token, however, homosexuality may not be thought of as particularly unusual in other cultures. To say that it is unnatural or immoral or repulsive is to impose a judgement upon it that has, according to this kind of theory, less to do with the reality of homosexuality than with the speaker's assumptions and the kinds of doctrine circulating in the culture.

It will by now have become apparent that the present book approaches the question of masculinity from the position of constructionist theory, which not only offers a less deterministic view of gender but also allows for a more interesting analysis of cultural conditions as they affect gender (and, it is worth noting, as they affect gender theory itself). And it is from this perspective that we return to the matter of the crisis in masculinity. The notion of a crisis presupposes that change is occurring in such a way as to cause discomfort and/or anxiety in those caught up in the change. However, to assume that masculinity has survived intact in its present form for centuries and is only now suffering unwelcome alteration is, at best, naive. History is more than a series of dates and facts: it is also the record of evolutions and revolutions in the culture. And all change potentially has an impact on issues pertaining to gender. It is the *mythology* of gender that struggles to remain stable by continuing to insist on a particular model or group of models of attitude and behaviour. (In structuralist and semiotic theory 'myth' signifies not falsehood, fable or legend but cultural belief. Thus science becomes one of the myths of our culture, not because it does not exist but because we use it to explain the world to ourselves. Myth makes sense of the universe to a particular culture.)

In the twentieth century the fact of two world wars (together with various extended minor wars and skirmishes, such as the Korean and the Vietnam actions) has had an important effect on the traditional, dominant model of masculinity. In each of these world wars the male populations of western societies were significantly reduced, requiring women to take on responsibilities and roles that hitherto had been the province of men. The case of World War II (1939–45) is particularly important in this regard. Servicemen who began returning from war in 1945 came back to a society in which women had endured various hardships such as food shortage as well as general privation, had survived bombing and bullets, and had learned to perform tasks that were dangerous—for instance, manufacturing armaments—or that required a certain amount of physical strength, stamina and mechanical know-how, such as running farms or operating factory equipment. To those soldiers it must have seemed that a radical revolution in femininity had taken place, and that women were no longer defenceless objects to be cherished and protected, as familiar gender definitions had taught. The men must also have feared that their strengths and skills as men might no longer be required; that, indeed, they had been emasculated by the very practice—war—which had traditionally allowed men to display masculine qualities such as courage, fortitude, endurance, stoicism and sheer physical strength.

Consequently, much of the popular literature and film produced in the late 1940s and the early 1950s stresses the normality of the traditional household, now that the men were coming back from the various fronts to which they had been posted. Women were no longer required to act like men; they could go back to being wives and mothers, needing comfort and protection. Ironically, it is the very emphasis on this re-establishment of the usual male–female relations and roles that causes one to enquire why it should be stated and restated repeatedly and so fervidly in those texts; and so one is led to perceive the fear that those narratives were intended to mask, namely, that the old way of life for men had been radically, irrevocably arrested and then altered.

It would, however, be erroneous to conclude that World War II should take all the credit for the contemporary interrogation of traditional masculinity. It had already begun earlier in the century. World War I (1914–18) was a major blow to the traditional imagery of war as heroic, glorious and especially as befitting young men. During this Great War, more young men died than in any previous war, and a generation of potentially brilliant writers, thinkers and scientists was grievously decimated. War, as fought in the trenches in the driving rain or snow of a European winter, was inglorious and dehumanising; mustard gas and other kinds of chemical warfare cut at the very heart of the idea of a chivalrous enemy whom one could see and with whom one could fight directly, as, indeed, also did the development of the submarine and the Zeppelin. In addition, the new phenomenon of shell-shock left men witless, amnesiac, nervous, prone to break down at the least noise or stress.

Indeed, as Elaine Showalter observes, military and medical authorities initially did not know whether to condemn the victims of this form of male hysteria for being unmanly or to sympathise with them and treat them with patience and consideration (see Showalter 1985:167–94). The term 'shell-shock' was coined because it was thought that the symptoms observed among cases of mental breakdown during the war resulted from the concussive effect of shells exploding near the soldiers, or from the chemical effects of such explosions (ibid.:167). In other words, the problem was thought to be physical or physiological, rather than emotional or psychological. Soldiers who fought in World War II and emerged with a similar syndrome were described as suffering from 'war neurosis', though this term was later changed to 'battle fatigue' in order to minimise the implications of actual illness, particularly in the United States, when large numbers of demoralised men returned from war. Likewise, 'post-traumatic stress disorder' described the effect of war on the psyches of the soldiers posted to Vietnam.[2] (What is interesting in these coinages is the attempt to focus on an *external* cause of the neurosis; by contrast, familiar terms for women's emotional or psychological disorders, like 'hysteria', for instance, locate the cause *within* the patient— 'hysteria' itself derives from the Greek word for 'womb'. Implicitly, then, men are not supposed to exhibit emotional upset or psychological disorder; but when they do, the fault is *around* them, not *in* them. Women, by contrast, then would seem to be *inherently* upset or disordered.)

Matters became the more perplexing because many soldiers whose actions were self-evidently courageous also suffered from battle neurosis. This in turn raised questions about the relation of traditional, abstract notions of manliness (which included stoicism in the face of pain) to the very real suffering of individual men who were the fathers, sons, brothers or friends of those at home. Dorothy L. Sayers, in creating Lord Peter Wimsey, the detective who figures in much of her fiction, identifies him both as a heroic soldier and a victim of shell-shock: the first Wimsey novel, *Whose Body?* (first published in 1923), contains a postscript written by Lord Peter's uncle, Paul Austin Delagardie, explaining that Lord Peter, having been disappointed in love, returned to the front in 1916

> with (I am sure) the fixed intention of getting killed; but all he got was his majority [that is, the rank of major] and his D.S.O. [Distinguished Service Order] for some recklessly good intelligence work behind the German front. In 1918 he was blown up and buried in a shell-hole near Caudry, and that left him with a bad nervous breakdown, lasting, on and off, for two years. (Sayers, 1973:188)

The same novel also contains a description of Lord Peter suffering from a nervous attack (ibid.:123–5). Interestingly, the effect of shell-shock here is both a symbol of the soldier's unmanning (he has to be comforted and put to bed by his man Bunter) and a confirmation of his courage in the line of duty. Indeed, one might even say that the latter meaning overwhelms and thus camouflages the former.

In this and other ways, the soldiers of the two world wars came to be represented popularly in film, literature and the media as either heroic and noble ('ours' or like 'us') or dastardly and cowardly ('theirs', or as good as): traditional notions of what it was to be a man had themselves taken a beating and needed to be reiterated and reinforced. Thus, for instance, the aerial dogfights became glamorised in later war nostalgia: superimposed upon the actual experiences of these soldiers were glorious mythic visions of medieval battles of knights on horseback, so that the fighters in their planes acquired the nimbus of the warriors of old, for whom questions about masculinity were not only unaskable but also unthinkable.

The aftermath of the war in the Great Depression of 1929 demolished another bulwark of the traditional model of masculinity, namely, employment. Waged labour became a key feature of this model in the late eighteenth century, with the advent of the industrial revolution and the changes that it effected in the lives of the middle and working classes. However, for our culture employment as a feature of masculinity has taken on the patina of a more venerable tradition, so that most people are unaware that modern patterns of employment are relatively recent. (The same is true of the apparently ages-old model of the nuclear family, and of modern notions of the child as a special, innocent individual: these concepts are in actual fact not much more than two hundred and fifty years old.) Like many men in the depressed economic climate of the late 1980s and early 1990s, men of the 1930s felt themselves to be less than 'real' men if they could not find jobs. Being able to support wives and families was a further burden for those who had spouses and children; but in the scale of our cultural values a man is more of a man if he has a job, and can demonstrate not only that he has necessary skills but also that he can be self-sufficient and independent of charity, whether from strangers or the state.

Another historical factor that has contributed to the destabilisation of the traditional concept of masculinity was the so-called sexual revolution, which, though largely a phenomenon of the 1960s, actually found its origins in the mid-1950s. Led by publications like *Playboy* magazine, and given a sort of manifesto by the pseudo-philosophical writing of *Playboy*'s founder and editor, Hugh Hefner, this revolution called men to throw off the shackles of traditional relationships, actualise their erotic fantasies, reject the dogmas of emotional and economic commitment to wife and family, and enjoy life hedonistically through the pleasures of transitory sexual entanglements and unashamed consumerism (see Ehrenreich, 1983:42–51). The sexual revolution thus enshrined the cultural myth of the sexually active male and made his practice— the continuing search for sexual conquests—an end in itself, cutting it free, moreover, from responsibility for the emotional, social and economic aspects of human relationships, the begetting and raising of children, and so on.

This sexual revolution intersected, in the 1960s, with the hippie movement and became part of a politics which radically challenged and flouted the conventions of an older generation that had led the younger into an apparently endless war in South-East Asia, into a Cold War with what used to be the Eastern Soviet bloc, and into the ever-present menace of devastating nuclear disaster. The return to a gentler ideology—'flower power'—was what the young now called for; and an effort was made to blur sexual difference by a 'unisex' creed, articulated especially through fashion in hairstyles and clothing. Sexual freedom was seen by the young as part of the idyllic return to nature as well as a means of shocking their elders. However, as a number of feminists have pointed out, the sexual freedom was really directed at males. Women were still expected to be sexually available to men but not necessarily to demonstrate any sexual initiative or desire that might upset the male's ego or his sense of sexual prowess. Nor could a woman require a man to commit himself to a long-term relationship with her, for this would infringe on his sexual freedom, contradicting the very ideology of the sexual revolution.

Hypocritical or prejudicial as this call for sexual revolution and freedom might have been, it had the effect of reinforcing one powerful belief about male sexuality, namely, that a man's sex drive is a potent force not to be obstructed lest detrimental physiological and psychological effects take place. We are probably all familiar with the adolescent male's rhetorical strategies to persuade young women to have sex with him; that, for instance, it will clear up his acne or that it will prevent some awful reaction caused by the penning up in his body of an excess of semen. These are simply immature versions of the dominant myth of male sexuality. One answer to all the stress and tribulation caused by enforced celibacy or sexual abstention is, of course, masturbation, which would surely also work wonders with acne, etc.; however, this is generally not the answer teenage boys—or, for that matter, many adult men—want to hear.

The appearance of HIV/AIDS in the early 1980s brought this era with its ideology of free and easy sex for all to a close. What had been the pursuit of erotic pleasure, it now appeared, might also be the fatal courting of a mysterious illness. Authorities counter-manded the dictates of the sexual revolution in two ways. Those concerned with guarding the morals of society, whether they were the spokespersons of various religious groups or self-appointed moral vigilantes, urged sexual abstinence or monogamous (hetero-sexual) union as the only alternatives to combat the epidemic. Sexual abstention was, however, precisely what the sexual revolu-tion had attempted to abolish, for it ran counter to the myth of the irresistible flood of male sexual desire.

Many health workers, by contrast, advised the practice of safe sex in casual and/or multiple sexual encounters and recommended commitment to long-term, stable relationships (whether hetero- or homosexual). The health worker's advice to the sexually active man that he use condoms as a safe-sex practice, however, seemed designed further to limit male sexuality. It was, moreover, a reminder of earlier birth-control practices which had become almost obsolete with the development in the 1960s of the birth-control pill. The Pill, as it became known, had offered a man a double advantage: first, he no longer had to fiddle, often embarrass-ingly, with a condom, and thus risk lowering the temperature of desire or inviting ridicule—he could, in short, have sex 'naturally'. Second, birth control became the woman's responsibility. Now, the safe-sex message was requiring him once again to start fiddling with condoms and to take responsibility, though perhaps of a different order and for a different reason, in matters of sex.

The HIV/AIDS epidemic thus has contributed to a revision of a notion of male sexuality as natural and free from responsibility. We should note, however, that this effect may not have brought about an immediate and marked change in the sexual practices of all members of society. For instance, some years after gay communities had taken on board the recommendation of various AIDS councils regarding safe-sex practices, the larger heterosexual community was still being targeted for safe-sex campaigns because its members, particularly the men, were slow to register that HIV/AIDS was not, as the media had first promoted it, an exclusively 'gay disease'. Similarly, there are some disturbing indications that even in the gay community there may now be a trend, especially among young men, back to the free-for-all sexual mores that obtained before the advent of HIV/AIDS. It may be that the young have become inured to the safe-sex message and now no longer hear it, or it may be that they assume that if they choose young men like themselves as their sexual partners, they will evade exposure to the virus from older, presumably more promiscuous men. Either way, the practice remains dangerous; and the second rationale has the unpleasant overtone of a sort of implicit genocidal programme whereby it is intended that older and possibly infected male homosexuals die out and take the virus with them. At any rate, it is likely that much of the vilification of gay men as the 'cause' of AIDS results from a refusal to accept that they may be merely one of the virus's initial vectors in the western world, a refusal which, in addition to a traditional hostility toward homosexuals, has at its base a strong resentment at the restricting of a male heterosexual practice that had been given licence for a couple of decades before HIV/AIDS appeared on the scene.

Against this historical background, we may identify two further, important events which had a powerful effect on cultural definitions of masculinity and of gender in general. First, there was the rise of various women's movements and of different kinds of feminism. It no longer makes much sense to speak of *the* women's movement or of an undifferentiated 'feminism': different cultures, nationalities, ethnicities and social classes have yielded different answers to questions like 'What does it mean to be a woman in this society?'. Those answers have necessarily contributed to different theorisations about feminism as a set of political strategies as well as a social theory or philosophy. However, feminist writing, of whatever political type or social stripe, has repeatedly emphasised that throughout history women have generally been subordinated—physically, sexually, domestically, socially, politically and economically—to men, though of course the nature and extent of that subordination has varied from culture to culture, and from one set of historical circumstances to another.

Sadness and anger have been the common responses by women to the idea that their history has been a tale of oppression by men, whether as individuals or as a class. The sadness has generally been shared with other women; the anger, however, has generally been directed at men, whose reaction has been variously puzzlement, perhaps patronising or indulgent amusement, but also often a reciprocal rage, part of what Susan Faludi (1992), Marilyn French (1992) and others have called the male backlash against feminism.

What is at stake here for men is not simply that they must now contend with women who refuse the place traditionally assigned to them or who, whether from motives of revenge or political opportunism, deny men sexual favours and hence jeopardise men's own sense of themselves as sexual beings. To see women's issues thus is to construct them as merely a modern variation of *Lysistrata* (411 BC). In this play, by the great Athenian comic playwright Aristophanes, the women of Athens decide to withhold sexual favours from their men until a pointless and destructive war in which the men are engaged is brought to an end. Needless, perhaps, to say, the women win; but this is a comedy, a genre which conventionally allowed the usual state of things to be turned upside down. In any case, the men's status *as men* is not really challenged in the play.

The challenge flung at men by modern feminism, however, is rather different. It has proven something of a conundrum for men. First, and very importantly, it has forced them willy-nilly to review their own positions and assumptions. Accusations by women of chauvinism, of injustice, of sexism on the part of the men with whom they come into daily contact—fathers, brothers, partners, sons, bosses, colleagues and friends—require those men to justify themselves even if that justification is merely a rejection of the charge. Moreover, a number of organisations, whether governmental or private and commercial, have for some time now brought in measures to rectify injustices against women perpetrated on the basis of sex alone and to ameliorate women's lot. These have included formal legislation for equal opportunity, the removal of discriminatory clauses, and official bans on sexist language. Regardless of whether these have been voluntary actions springing from a true sense of justice for all or have been the effect of pressure by women's lobby groups, they have necessarily modified male behaviour to a greater or lesser extent. For their part, men may feel such measures to be only fair and just or, on the contrary, they may feel put upon and persecuted by women; but in any case they have been forced to define themselves against women in ways that are, for our culture at any rate, quite novel. Until quite recently men's superiority and hence their dominance over women have gone unquestioned, indeed have frequently been thought natural and even universal and therefore beyond question.

Second, and related to the foregoing, the challenge of feminism creates a critical and tactical dilemma for men: how should they respond to feminism/activist women? Should they respond at all—would it be manly to do so? Would it be more seemly if men in fact refused the challenge? Or should men fly in the face of gender tradition and accept women as equals, with all that this implies and requires, personally, psychologically, emotionally, sexually, socially?

The conventional joke about the war between the sexes thus often seems, to many men, not to be a joke any more. It would appear that the divide sundering the sexes grows wider, particularly when men are broadly labelled by many women as the enemy. Men thus find themselves removed from their traditional role as protectors of womankind, and placed instead in the paradoxical position of reviled antagonists held at bay by a contingent of women who define themselves as men's victims, but who, as victims, seem ironically to have turned feral. The situation is of course intensified by a separatist feminist politics which constructs men not only as the enemy but as an irrelevancy to the concerns and lives of women.

There have been two general classes of response to these developments in feminism and in women's changing attitudes toward men. The first has been a reaction of anger and violence. In its most fundamental form, this has meant a strengthening of men's conventional attitudes toward women and an attempt to reimpose the traditional control of women, often phrased, in the language of politicians and moralists (not always identical with each other) as 'traditional family values', which include the nuclear family as the ideal, in which the husband and father goes out to work while the wife and mother stays home to take care of their house and two-point-something children.[3]

A more elaborated version of this kind of response has been the call issued by some men to all other men to rediscover their inner, primitive masculinity. This idea is fraught with theoretical and philosophical problems, beginning, of course, with the notion that there *is* some central, fundamental 'essence' or reality of masculinity. Robert Bly's myth of Iron John is perhaps the representative instance of this reaction. *Iron John: A Book About Men* (1991) is an amalgam of anthropology, myth, poetry, psychology, and autobiography which, while agreeing that women have been oppressed by men and required to serve men all their lives, also in some ways blames women for men's loss of the sense of their own masculinity. Bly is famous now for instituting programmes in which groups of men meet in the woods to rediscover the Wild Man apparently within all men. His ideas and programmes have proven popular both in North America and elsewhere, including Australia. However, while the Iron John project may be seen at one level as a perhaps important effort to enable men to readjust their values in the face of changing relations between the sexes and to encourage them to discover other, 'softer', more emotional facets of themselves, at another level there is an underlying separatist current to which many men have responded by affirming vehemently their need to be with other men (not necessarily for sex) and their ability to dispense with their former need of women.

The other class of response assumes men's affirmation of women's claims. Into this category fall the responses which David Morgan labels the penitential and the petitional:

> The penitential (often adopting a confessional mode) may include a recognition of the wrongs that men have done to women, both in general terms and often in particular terms with reference to the experiences or past practices of the writer. (Morgan, 1992:38)

In considering the alternative mode, the petitional, we are considering the way in which men might come to a realization of the damage done to themselves in the context of a patriarchal society. These may be generalized damages, such as stifling of the authentic expression of feelings or taboos on tenderness, or particular damages such as those faced by non-conformist men, gays, effeminate or sensitive men, non-athletic men and so on. (Ibid.:40)[4]

Such responses need to be examined carefully. As Morgan points out, men do not come to the issue of gender politics from the same position as women. They are usually already empowered in certain ways. The guilt experienced and expressed by a man, whether concerning his own individual behaviour or that of his entire sex, may often be seasoned with a certain complacency or satisfaction. These, in turn, are grounded in the fact that, as a man, he enjoys a certain power and luxury which enable him to meditate on and articulate that guilt. It is, if one likes, the aristocrat's twinge of conscience for the defeated existence of his labouring, suffering peasantry: it does not necessarily lead him to give up his rank, wealth, power and privilege.

Nor is the power that men enjoy in our culture easily to be surrendered, given away or abdicated from. Aside from the seductions and advantages of such power, the censure which the individual man would incur from other men often acts as a sufficient deterrent to any real surrender of power. For a man publicly and unmistakably to give up his claim to masculine power and privilege may be to invite not only the disapproval of other men but also their violence. This has frequently been the experience of gay men, who are generally perceived as failures in terms of dominant notions of masculinity.

This is not to say that there is nowhere a man who genuinely wishes to step outside the patriarchal dynamics required of all men in our culture, or who wishes to improve the lot of women. But political correctness, however authentically desired or sincerely voiced, may nevertheless mask, even from the individual himself, his maintenance of the status quo. Thus the politically correct New Age Man (or SNAG: Sensitive New Age Guy, as he is sometimes also called), supposedly more sensitive to women's needs both personal and political, more self-aware ('self-realised') and more honouring of the earth and of nature than his fellows who pillage their environment for power and profit—this new breed of man is often regarded suspiciously by women and men alike. For women, the question is, can the leopard change its spots? Or, to employ another cliché, is New Age Man really the same old wolf decked out in new sheep's clothing? Is his new-found sensitivity and so on merely a strategy to keep things as they are, allowing him to continue to prey sexually on women? For some men, on the other hand, New Age Man may appear to be a wimp, a man who has sold to women his birthright as a male.

For many men the claims and challenges of women seem to have created a labyrinth without exit. Attacked by feminism, whether as theory or as political action, and denied their traditional preroga-tives, especially of power and sexuality, many men feel resentful toward women. Others may feel that though they are willing at least to try and be unconventional in taking up a pro-feminist position, they may lose more than they gain by incurring ridicule, derision, hostility and even violence from other men. Furthermore, this state of affairs is likely to breed, on the one hand, a cyni-cism which encourages men to be in turn the traditional macho individual and the newer sensitive one, as circumstances require; and, on the other, confusion and despair about how to behave as a man.

A second, important factor contributing to the critical re-exami-nation of masculinity has been made by the thought and writing of gay politics. Gay liberation, like women's liberation, emerged in the late 1960s and in many ways bore similarities to women's liberation. Gays, like women, are a marginalised group and, like women, have been oppressed. They have also been openly persecuted, whether within or outside formal legal process. Both groups, therefore, are positioned to examine critically the dynamics by which they are marginalised and oppressed, dynamics emerging out of traditional notions of masculinity.

Many gay historians identify the critical moment for gay libera-tion as the Stonewall episode of 27–30 June 1969, when gay men in the Stonewall Inn in Greenwich Village, New York City, unexpectedly erupted in anger at police harassment, which had become routine for twenty years (see Warren Johansson, 'Stonewall

Rebellion', in Dynes, 1990). The effect of the Stonewall Rebellion or Riot, as it came to be called, was far-reaching. It demonstrated that gays were no longer willing to be pushed around and forced into the shadows, a demonstration which in turn provided the impetus for many homosexuals to 'come out of the closet'.[5] Significantly, the incident also gave to homosexuals a radical political edge different from the conciliatory politics of existing homophile (that is, gay-oriented) organisations like the Mattachine Society. From Stonewall and from similar episodes elsewhere in the United States and in Europe, the Gay Liberation Front (GLF) was born and spread also to England and Australia (see Adam, 1987:75–101).

Though rivalry with other gay movements, together with internal differences, eventually brought about its demise, as a political entity the GLF had a radical programme: not only to fight for the rights of homosexuals but also to provide a critical analysis of social prejudice and injustice. The early gay rights movement thus had much in common with women's issues, though a decade later these two groups had moved apart, each with a different agenda. Many women, both heterosexual and homosexual, began to feel that gay men were not so very different from their straight brethren in their concentration on sexual conquest; many women, too, began to feel that gay men were more interested in becoming accepted as men by male heterosexuals than in the plight of the oppressed in general, including straight and gay women, and the politics implied thereby. And women also began to perceive an element of misogyny (woman-hatred) in gay men's dealings with women. Many lesbians therefore decided to throw their lot in with the women's movements rather than with the gay movement, now seen as committed principally to gay *men*'s causes rather than to those of gay *people*. Indeed, more and more the word 'gay' by itself came to connote 'male homosexual'.

We might observe here that female homosexuality in any case has rarely been taken seriously by men in western patriarchal cultures. In Britain, for instance, the Labouchère Amendment of 1885 imposed a maximum two-year prison term, with or without hard labour, for a man judged guilty of 'an act of gross indecency' with another man, regardless of whether that act was performed in public or in private. It proved influential also in Australian legal attitudes to male homosexuality. The Wolfenden Committee in Britain recommended in 1957 the repeal of this clause of criminal law (see 'Criminal Law Amendment Act' in Dynes, 1990).

The passing into law of the Labouchère Amendment, which was responsible for the conviction of Oscar Wilde in 1895, did not extend to homosexual activity between women. According to legend, Queen Victoria refused to believe that women would engage in such activity (though apparently she had less difficulty in believing that men did), and hence refused to sign a bill outlawing lesbian sexuality. Jeffrey Weeks, however, observes that it was not until 1921 that Parliament attempted to extend criminal law to lesbian sexual activity (Weeks, 1977:106); even so, the attempt was unsuccessful. Thus female homosexuality has never been regarded as criminal, though it may have often been seen as unusual or abnormal. Moreover, lesbian sex has often been eroticised for and by heterosexual males, and thus can be deprived of its meaning and value as a sexual activity between women only.

In the late 1980s, nevertheless, under the pressure of the AIDS crisis, lesbians and gay men effected a narrowing of the political gap which divided the two groups. This occurred partly out of sympathy for those ill with the virus, and the need to establish a system of support for PLWAs (people living with AIDS), most of whom, certainly until 1990, were gay men. But it also came about because of powerful anti-homosexual pressures from right-wing political elements who sought to reimpose archaic laws, restrictions and penalties upon homosexuals and who justified such regressive action by reference to the AIDS crisis. Though male homosexuals were the chief target here, there might be repercussions for the lesbian community.

The political and social writing coming out of the gay movement raises questions about the binary system instituted through dominant notions of masculinity and femininity, whereby individuals must fit into either/or categories of male/female, heterosexual/homosexual, active/passive, and so on. It challenges the right of men to assume superiority over women and of heterosexual men to assume superiority over homosexuals. It questions stereotypes of male homosexuals as effeminates and provides information about homosexuals and homosexuality to replace the gossip, slander, fable and misinformation that underlie much anti-homosexual prejudice. It has also provided manifestos and theorisations of political and social action on the part of gays (and lesbians), such as the phenomenon of radical or gender-fuck drag of the 1970s, in which men dressed in women's clothing but with no attempt to impersonate women, so that obviously male facial and body hair remained to contradict the female attire. (This found a certain analogue in the 1980s with 'gender-bending' pop stars like Boy George and Marilyn.) Such acts—which often outraged straight onlookers—demonstrated that gender is visually constructed by social and cultural codes like dress or physical appearance, rather than by any innate femininity or masculinity.

Out of the challenges offered to men by history and the critique of masculinity (developed on the one hand by feminist theory, and on the other by gay political theory) has come a fracturing of 'masculinity' as an integrated concept. Of course, men have never conformed universally to any such concept. We might, therefore, say that there have always been many masculine *identities*, if by this we understand not only that men have always been heterosexual, homosexual, macho, effeminate, pro-woman, anti-woman and so on, but also that individual men have always had different life-experiences *as men*. Now, however, the overriding cultural myth of a single masculinity appears to be cracking and splitting, allowing various *masculinities* to emerge.

But this is not to say that the older notion of masculinity has disappeared. As we noted earlier, myths of gender can be very persistent, and certainly many men feel that they have much to lose in acquiescing to the idea that masculinity is not, as they have been taught, a single set of ways of thinking and behaving. However, the emphatic assertion of that model today suggests sometimes that it is undertaken in a defensive posture, and that defensiveness partly defines the crisis in which masculinity finds itself.

From this situation has emerged a relatively new field of study: the theory of masculinity, also sometimes called the new men's studies. 'Masculinism' (or more properly 'masculism', by analogy with 'feminism') has not found much support, perhaps because it suggests a reactionary assertion of traditional ideas about masculinity, including the subordination of women and the marginalisation of gays. The study of men and masculinity is not especially recent: for instance, in the United States, *Men and Masculinity*, edited by Joseph H. Pleck and Jack Sawyer, appeared in 1974, and presented a variety of sociological, psychological and confessional writing, while Andrew Tolson's *The Limits of Masculinity*, which emerged from the author's work with the Birmingham Men's Group in Britain, was published in 1977 and is an important early examination of men's issues. *In Rediscovering Masculinity: Reason, Language and Sexuality* Victor J. Seidler (1989) provides an account of the men's groups like Red Therapy in the 1970s in Britain which sought to explore questions of men's emotions and sexuality and relationships with women as a way of complementing the consciousness-raising experience that enabled many of their women friends and partners to develop as individuals. This period also saw the rise of *Achilles Heel*, a magazine dedicated to the exposition and analysis of men's issues in the light of feminism (see Seidler, 1991a, 1992). In Britain the exploration of masculinity has thus been undertaken for around twenty years; and it is characteristically Marxist in its assumptions and its approach, that is, it is concerned to explore political, historical and economic dimensions of culture and gender. (Tim Carrigan, Bob Connell and John Lee provide a useful history of both the concerns and the writing of the emergent field of men's studies in Carrigan et al., 1987.)

What is quite new, however, is the shift of the study of men's issues from the relative privacy of men's groups to the more public domain of the universities. The late 1980s, for instance, saw a parallel to the earlier setting up of women's studies courses in the establishment of men's studies courses at a number of American universities by, among others, Michael S. Kimmel of the Department of Sociology at the State University of New York at Stony Brook, and Michael A. Messner of the Program for the Study of Women and Men in Society and the Department of Sociology at the University of Southern California. Indeed, Jeff Hearn and David Morgan note that 'a recent report suggests that by the end of 1989 there were more than two hundred courses "dealing with some aspect of the male experience" in colleges and universities in the United States' ('Men, Masculinities and Social Theory' in Hearn and Morgan, 1990:18, note 2). In his important collection of essays on masculinity, *The Making of Masculinities: The New Men's Studies*, Harry Brod outlines the intellectual and political concerns for the emergent field of men's studies (see Brod, 1987:1–17 and 39–62).

In Australia, the institutionalisation of men's studies remains in its infancy (one is tempted to say 'boyhood'): aside from the occasional semester-long programme at one or two universities, the study of men and masculinity has generally been restricted to component status in courses in women's studies or gender theory, located in various disciplines, ranging from literature through film studies to sociology. Outside the academies there is evidence of quite a lot of interest in men's issues: men's groups have been established in most of the States, and there is a national magazine, *XY: Men, Sex, Politics*, devoted to the dissemination of information pertinent to men and to the discussion of a range of issues. The magazine announces that it 'affirms a healthy, life-loving, non-oppressive masculinity, and supports the men's networks for change in Australia. *XY* is a space for the exploration of issues of gender and sexuality, and practical discussion of the hows and whys of personal and social change. *XY* is male-positive, pro-feminist and gay-affirmative'.

There have also been attempts both in Australia and overseas to institute gay and lesbian studies, a move which has perhaps inevitably met with resistance from some quarters of the academic establishment, though research into questions of gender makes it clear that studies of masculinity and femininity, as well as of male and female sexuality, cannot be seriously undertaken without proper consideration also of issues surrounding male and female homosexuality. The institution in 1993 of the Australian Centre for Gay and Lesbian Research, located at the University of Sydney, is the first national and formal recognition in Australia of the need for such research.

The academicising of men's issues has generally been led by several disciplines, chief among them sociology and psychology. In recent years, the theory of masculinity has also been taken up by cultural studies, which as a multi-disciplinary approach permits the application of sociological and psychological theory to various kinds of cultural text, ranging from print to electronic media, and including 'lived' texts such as architectural design, clothing fashion and the like, while at the same time exploring how masculinity is represented in such texts.

For some, courses in men's studies may seem like gilding the lily since in one way or another men have always been at the centre of cultural preoccupations. For others, such courses are a way for men to make their various voices heard. This is important for two reasons. First, it identifies male experiences and perspectives as *not* equivalent to all human experience and perspectives (as the generic 'he', 'man' or 'mankind' suggest); second, it indicates that the experiences of individual men are not all the same. Also important is the fact that men's studies enables the student to arrive at an understanding about how men think and function and respond— to events, to other men, to women. This has, in the past, generally been silenced, or acknowledged only with some embarrassment, since to permit such an understanding has been to make men vulnerable, to other men as well as to women. Such study, moreover, also has the potential to enable men to change patterns and habits of thinking and behaving which have often been as damaging to them as to the women around them, and which we will explore in the next chapter through a reading of Béla Bartók's opera *Duke Bluebeard's Castle*.

'Light must end the reign of darkness': Manning the Ramparts

The story of Bluebeard is an old one. The historical Bluebeard, Gilles de Retz (or Rais; 1404–40), a companion-at-arms of Joan of Arc, later a would-be alchemist and dabbler in the black arts, then arrested and charged for sexual assault on and murder of children on his domain, was by the time of Charles Perrault's tale in the late seventeenth century transformed into the wife-murdering ogre with whom we are familiar today. In the various versions of this story since Perrault, the focus is usually on the wife as victim (or near-victim, since she escapes her husband's clutches in most retellings of the plot). However, the form taken by the tale in Bartók's opera *Duke Bluebeard's Castle* by contrast focuses instead on Bluebeard himself, and in so doing invites us to consider the story differently.

The play *Bluebeard's Castle* (in Hungarian, *A kékszakállú herceg vára*) was written by Béla Balázs a few years before it was submitted to Bartók as a possible opera libretto (Zoltán Kodály was another composer to whom Balázs considered offering the libretto). Completed in 1911, the opera was first performed in 1918. On 15 November 1930, however, Balázs wrote a letter to Bartók renouncing his claim to credit for the opera (Demény, 1971:198). (Both for this reason, and for clarity's sake, I shall refer to the author of the libretto as Bartók, even though the musical structure of the opera is not the focus of the present discussion).[1]

Duke Bluebeard's Castle is set in neither a specific historical period nor a specific geographical location; and there are only two singing parts in it—the three remaining roles are mute. It is a fantasy narrative which commences with the return of Bluebeard and his bride Judith to the Duke's castle, of which we see only a dark, Gothic hall without windows, containing a staircase and seven doors (excluding the one through which Bluebeard and Judith enter). Judith, appalled by the cheerlessness of Bluebeard's home, wants to let light in, as she says, to 'end the reign of darkness'.[2] The plot is apparently motivated by Judith's desire to find out all about her husband and his life, which she effects through her insistence that she be given the keys to the doors so that she can find out what lies behind each.

However, where Judith is eager to explore and expose the contents of the seven chambers, Bluebeard is reluctant to allow her to do so. It is only under pressure from her that he hands the keys over, repeatedly begging her to refrain from satisfying her curiosity; but she insists, and one by one the doors are opened, disclosing to her (and to us) what lies behind them. When Bluebeard demonstrates extreme unwillingness to relinquish the last key, Judith excitedly surmises that the corpses of his murdered former wives are kept in this seventh chamber. Again Bluebeard surrenders the key and Judith finds that the wives are indeed there; but they are alive. No sooner has she discovered this than Bluebeard robes and crowns her regally like the others and compels her to enter the seventh chamber with the other three women. The bleak Duke remains alone, gradually engulfed in the darkness that sweeps across the stage.

The choice of an opera as a text suitable for a reading from the perspective of gender, and especially of masculinity, may seem a bit idiosyncratic or capricious. However, gender dynamics and politics may be found to underlie even the unlikeliest text although, because they are often taken for granted, they may become invisible. Thus such issues may be found woven into the fabric even of sociology texts, as Morgan (1992) demonstrates, though one might have thought such works would be 'scientific', that is, neutral and objective. Morgan shows, in his reading of Max Weber's *The Protestant Ethic and the Spirit of Capitalism* (1904–05) and of William Foote Whyte's *Street Corner Society* (1955), how many of the authors' observations are grounded in masculine views of society, and of social interaction, and hence in certain assumptions and biases (ibid.:49–71).

In the case of *Duke Bluebeard's Castle*, it becomes clear (in Judith's insistence that the chambers be opened, and in Bluebeard's reluctant granting of permission) that certain gender issues and conflicts are being enacted and that the castle may be best understood as a metaphor for Bluebeard's own identity.[3] One way of reading this text from the perspective of gender is to see Judith either as an inexperienced young woman or as a very inquisitive wife (these are not mutually exclusive, merely different possibilities) who, whether from the best or the worst of motives, thrusts her way into her husband's inner life and for her pains is forced to go the way of the other women in Bluebeard's life. Whether as an audience we are made to feel that this serves her right or that, a victim, she is forced to act in a scenario not of her own writing, will depend both on what (gender) presuppositions we bring to the opera and on how the opera is actually performed. The same is true about whether Bluebeard is understood to be a victim of his own failure to reach out to others or whether he is represented as a sort of generic male with a private, inviolable inner life, something that women seem unable to grasp, wanting instead to rip aside its defences and expose it to view. In the second possibility, it is Woman (and not just Judith—we assume that the other wives made the same error) who fails Man.

These are possible preferred readings of the text and are elaborated by a number of commentators on the opera. For instance, David Ewen, in his *Encyclopedia of the Opera* (1955), says simply that 'the story of Bluebeard and his last wife, Judith . . . is the basis of a psychological text emphasizing the eternal conflict between man and woman'. This summary takes for granted a perpetual gender conflict, which the opera simply reproduces. By contrast, in the *Concise Oxford Dictionary of Opera* (1972) Harold Rosenthal and John Warrack tell us that the story is that of 'a sorrowing, idealistic man who takes Judith . . . his newest bride, home to his murky castle. She makes him unlock his secret doors one by one and when she has penetrated his innermost secret she takes her place, another failure, among the other wives behind the last door, leaving Bluebeard in his loneliness'. This brief account leaves it ambiguous whether Judith is 'another failure' because she is the wrong wife for Bluebeard, that is, he chose unwisely, so the failure is his; or because Judith, like Bluebeard's other wives (and, by implication, all other women), does not know how to behave as a successful partner to Bluebeard. József Ujfalussy suggests that Bluebeard 'personifies the tragedy of man's impenetrable solitariness' ('man' here seems to be a generic term for 'people', not for 'men'). That Ujfalussy sees the opera's theme as a general one for everybody is made clear in his further comment that 'Balázs interprets the legend to signify that we are ourselves Bluebeards held captive in the castle of our irrational fears, robber barons every one, building a home for ourselves out of the souls, tears and blood of others from whom we have stolen their treasures', to be released by the love and self-sacrifice of another (Ujfalussy, 1971:107–8). Paul Griffiths, on the other hand, reads the opera as an individual tragedy: 'it is not at all clear whether Bluebeard begins with the idea that he can enjoy a new, untainted life with Judith provided he keeps his past a secret, or whether he knows himself all along to be the victim of an inevitable cycle in which his wife will come to know him and therefore be lost to him' (1984:61). The patently symbolic nature of the Duke's castle, however, allows us to read the opera not only as the account of the failure of an individual relationship between a man and a woman but also as an allegory (an extended metaphor) about masculinity itself.

In the preceding chapter, we considered how cultural models of gender govern the way in which we accept or reject certain attitudes and behaviours as appropriate to a particular gender identity. We need now to consider how that regulation takes place. Earlier we noted that certain codes in the culture determine how men and women behave differently. Now we can elaborate that idea to say that these codes carry not only general *meaning* (this is how a man behaves, this is how a woman behaves), but also *power significa-tion* (this is how a man controls, this is how a woman controls) and *valorisations* (such a behaviour is good or bad, better or worse, inferior or superior). Taken together, these constitute a *discourse* of gender.

A discourse may be thought of as a kind of language about a topic or preoccupation in the culture. Its 'vocabulary' is not only verbal (that is, the words available, and what is actually said) but also behavioural and gestural signs (what physical action, clothing, behaviour and so on are permitted or deemed appropriate). And its 'grammatical' rules define who can speak, who can be spoken to, and what can be 'said', as well as who and what must remain silenced. Discourses thus impose limits and establish relations of power within the culture; and we all learn them, even though they may restrict or deprive us in certain ways. They contribute to how we are defined in the culture and how we may act (and speak) acceptably and appropriately. They also provide us with the very mechanisms by which we view the world, interpret and 'think' it.

If issues of power—which include empowerment of some and the disempowerment of others implicated in the discourse—are involved, discourses are not and cannot be neutral. To begin with, because of the question of social power they necessarily reflect particular aspects of politics in the society and, more generally, of various cultural ideologies. Thus, in addition to defining what can be said, discourses also reflect dominant cultural preoccupations and limitations with regard to what is said and to whom; and with regard to who is to be 'heard' and thus empowered by being given a voice, and who is to be silenced and hence disempowered. Discourses which articulate preferences and preoccupations saturating the culture thus generally appear to be inevitable and natural. Such may be called *dominant* discourses.

However, no discourse is of itself 'natural' or inevitable, though it is the task of ideology to make it seem so. Society is made up of a diversity of people with many needs, experiences, behaviours and attitudes. There are, therefore, many discourses operating in the culture, and the presence of any one discourse or kind of discourse necessarily means that other possible discourses (which may offer different positions and relations of power) have been excluded or temporarily jostled away. If those privileged or preferred by the culture are dominant discourses, we may think of these others as *alternative* or *oppositional* discourses. We might, moreover, also distinguish notionally between an inclusive *master discourse*, such as that of gender, and a *component discourse*, such as the discourse of masculinity or of femininity.

An example would probably help at this point. Not so very long ago, a wife could not protest officially that she had been raped by her husband or had been subjected to violence by him: such claims were regarded as fanciful or exaggerated, or they were character- ised as the ravings of a neurotic female. Besides, did not husbands legally have control over their wives? In any case, who ever heard of rape within marriage, a condition of living undertaken *voluntar- ily* not only by the husband but also by the wife? And so a discourse which privileged men over women and effectively permitted violence to be enacted by men toward women silenced the battered, raped and otherwise maltreated wife. In addition, it reinforced that silence by threatening her with ridicule (she became that object of scorn and figure of many jokes, the neurotic female) or with censure (she was perceived as not properly obedient to her husband and therefore as not loving him sufficiently, or not being 'womanly' enough—that is, socially and sexually compliant). It could also impose on her a legal coercion (rape was not a legally viable concept in relation to marriage; the law required the wife's submission to the husband's authority; and so on). It is this discourse which in January 1993 underlay a judicial ruling in a case in South Australia that some 'rougher than usual handling' must be expected where a husband required sexual relations from his wife. Though this observation may have been cited out of context in media reports, it understandably stirred up a storm of outraged protest all over Australia, since it reinvoked that discourse and gave it the credibility of a decision in law.

This particular discourse, which we may describe as a marital, gender-political one, also demonstrates how discourses frequently intersect with and converge upon one another. Few discourses stand alone: they often function alongside or are involved in others. Here, some of the other discursive elements implicated in such a situation are those which characterise males not only as physically strong but as licensed to use that strength on others; those which see women as part of the goods and chattels of their men, who may dispose of their belongings as they wish; and those which define women as intellectually and morally inferior to men and thence requiring men to show them the 'right way' to do things, a process which might require coercion where persuasion does not work; and so on.

Alternative but uninvoked elements of the discourse might have been those which characterise husbands who use force on their wives as sexually incompetent (they are not seductive enough or are poor performers in bed, so that their wives are not attracted to them 'naturally'—a question of sexual adequacy or expertise);[4] or as brutes barely evolved from the apes (this perspective frequently has class or race bias, so that the man to whom it is applied may be seen as no better than he should be because he is 'only' working-class, or 'only' black, or possibly a genetic throwback who knows no better); or as a boor without civilised habits (this view derives from a romantic facet of the discourse of gender which requires men to exercise chivalry toward the 'weaker' sex). Discursive options at present utterly alien to our culture might also have been invoked, for instance that women are sacred beings and are defiled by the touch of men (such an option might carry a death penalty as a deterrent to any future sacrilege). These optional discourses, which do not throw a particularly good light on men (but some of which, we might note in passing, generally tend to exonerate the male as congenitally or naturally incapable of other behaviour) were clearly excluded in the case of the judge's decision in the South Australian case.

Discourses which foreground men's needs, men's privilege and men's power are often described, especially in women's writing, as *phallocentric* (phallocentrism is discussed further in Chapter 4) and are a feature of a society which is *patriarchal* in structure. The passing of the term 'patriarchy' into common parlance has resulted in the occasional distortion of its meaning so that it signifies merely 'of or pertaining to men'. We should recall, however, that 'patriarchy' does have a precise sociological and anthropological sense, namely, a social structure ruled or dominated by the oldest man in the group (the patriarch), who is often thought of and sometimes even addressed as the people's father, though this may be a symbolic or honorific, and not necessarily an actual, relationship. Within this social structure the patriarch controls the structure and distribution of power, frequently through his authority over the women of the tribe and how they are disposed of to the men. That is, the patriarch controls the men of the tribe by controlling how the women are to be distributed and who obtains them. An important point here, and one that is frequently lost or ignored in discussion, is that in traditional patriarchies power is not shared equally by all men in the group.

In feminist thought, 'patriarchy' has come to signify the domination of society by men and their values. Such a state of affairs inevitably operates to advantage men and to disadvantage women. 'Patriarchy' has come also to indicate what we may call a macro-discourse of masculinity, so that 'patriarchy' and 'masculinity' often become conflated. In philosophical terms, 'masculinity' would appear to be the more inclusive category; 'patriarchy' then becomes a type or form or expression of masculinity. However, there is scant anthropological or archaeological evidence for the existence of matriarchal cultures, which seems to imply, as much feminist writing suggests, that all human societies may have emerged from patriarchal origins. This in turn implies that 'patriarchy' is the inclusive term since it would condition all forms of masculinity. Nevertheless, anthropologists have found that notions of the masculine and of appropriately masculine behaviour are not uniform in all racial or ethnic communities, which would seem to leave the question open. Whether 'patriarchy' is a subset of 'masculinity' or vice versa is an interesting problem we must leave aside in the present discussion. In any event, 'patriarchy' has become a rather vague term, indicating an ideological (rather than an actual social) pattern directing the way in which men and women are constructed and how power is distributed in the culture. But we should note that though the term itself may have become somewhat blurred in meaning, the *effects* of a patriarchal social structure (in the feminist sense) are nevertheless real, and damaging to both women and men.

In modern, western patriarchal society, as in traditional tribal ones, there is a differential power relationship among the men. In our culture, however, power is generally diffuse, and accesses to power (and the ways in which power itself may be wielded) are highly varied and often not clearly defined. Thus, though men may all have been born male, they do not therefore, in our patriarchal society, automatically possess equal power, any more than all the men in traditional patriarchies do. Access to power may be correlated, among other things, with such factors as physical build and strength, age, (official) sexual orientation and prowess (even if only rumoured), social class and advantage, economic power, race of the individual, and so on. To men, the stratification of this power and privilege within patriarchal structures is very apparent. From the macho football hero to the mousy accountant who is thought to be gay, from the middle-aged international businessman to the young plumber's apprentice or the Aboriginal man in jail for vagrancy, men are aware of being defined as having more or less power, of being central within the system or marginal to it. Moreover, men are also aware that the privileged, desirable positions within patriarchal structures are often held only provisionally, and that the tenants of those positions may be displaced by rivals who may be younger, stronger, sexier, more authoritative or whatever. We should note, though, that the patriarchal process of installing and then removing occupants of a particular empowered position is not, of course, limited to men. Women have experienced similar control in patriarchal operations and preferences. Much feminist writing in fact deals with the patriarchal manipulation of women in the culture.

Those positions and any changes to their tenancy are decided by other men, not necessarily through any formal conclave of elders or of peers, but rather through the attitude and behaviour of other males, which are in turn regulated by the circulation of dominant discourses. These lay down the current orthodoxy of gender behaviour. The rules of gender behaviour are thus often vague, and learned mostly by observation and imitation rather than through direct instruction. For all their lack of clear definition, however, those rules operate decisively, so that individual men not favoured by other men in the patriarchal stakes are quite conscious of lack of support by other men or of being marginalised by them. And this process begins quite early—even in the school playground: the boy who is inept on the sportsfield or the kid who is thought to be too quiet or effeminate both know when the support of other males has been withdrawn from them so that they are relegated to the margins of the male world they inhabit. The same is true of the man excluded from the male camaraderie at the local pub or treated as different, not quite 'one of the boys', because of his social position, his sexual orientation, his taste in clothes, or because of his lack of 'leadership quality', aggression or 'drive'. These latter qualities, however indistinct, are often referred to by the idiomatic term 'balls', as in 'He's got a lot of balls'. We might note here the fusion of genital formation—balls or testicles—with social behaviour so that aggressive conduct, whether on the football field, in the business boardroom or on the street, is identified not only with masculinity but also with male (hetero)sexuality.

The supervision by males of other males under patriarchy generates a paradoxical condition of existence for men. On the one hand, they find themselves in competition with men from a very early age; indeed, if we accept Freud's theory of the Oedipal phase of infantile sexuality, such competition begins when the boy is a baby and finds himself rivalling his father for the attention and love (and sexuality, according to Freud) of his mother. In this way, the young male learns early that all other males are potential rivals and enemies and that if he wants a place in the patriarchal sun, he must outdo or conquer these others. We might think of this state of affairs as the Masculinity Stakes, a race or competition in which only winners count.

On the other hand, he also learns that though women, beginning with his mother and including female friends and various sexual partners, might *confirm* his masculinity, it is other men who *confer* it upon him. To be called a 'sissy' or told that he runs or throws a ball 'like a girl' is a dreadful insult to a boy: in the first place, it is usually other males who offer it and, in the second place, it means that other males as a group effectively deny him his claim to masculinity. From here it is only a short step to being labelled a homosexual ('fag', 'fairy', 'poofter' and so on do not simply name a sexual orientation but also identify it as non-normative, hence marginal and inviting insult and hostility). Thus commences a conflictive and troublesome relationship with other members of his sex that often produces high anxiety in the male, in that he must compete with others and yet seek their companionship if he wishes to be part of that group called '(real) men'. The tension and dynamics thus produced can affect males both in hierarchical relationships (for instance, between father and son, teacher and student, boss and worker) and in relationships of nominal equality (for instance, between brothers, friends and colleagues).

It also results in a gender existence in which the individual man feels that he is constantly being watched by other men and that any slips or falterings in the patterns of behaviour broadly labelled 'masculine' are noted. Under such a condition of surveillance many men may feel that, after a particular (but never specified) number of (often also unspecified) errors, they will be publicly humiliated by other men and deprived of their gender status *as men*. So many will strive for a hypermasculinity, that is, an excessive masculinity, whether signified by a huge, muscular body, an impressive sexual scorecard (which may not bear any relation to reality—here, as in other aspects of masculine behaviour, it is the reputation which is important, not the actuality), a powerful car or a high-flying job. Nor should we exclude men's acts of violence toward women and children, and other men, especially gays, as an attempt to assert their masculinity in the eyes of their fellows. Such aggression is often explained, in essentialist gender theory, as the result of testosterone levels in the individual man. Though this male hormone certainly seems implicated in acts of male aggression and violence, it cannot surely be the sole cause; nor does this hypothesis satisfactorily explain acts of female aggression and violence, which, even if much rarer, nevertheless do take place. Constructionist theory, by contrast, seeks to identify the relationship between testosterone-induced aggression and the *meaning* it has in patriarchal culture, together with the *use* to which it may be put. These often give signals to males in the culture that it is or is not all right to vent aggression.

Because of such dynamics as the often unstated rivalry among men, their surveillance and sometimes suspicion of one another, and their fear of being identified—or even only labelled—as homosexual by their fellow men, Eve Kosofsky Sedgwick argues, male–male relationships in our culture are generally discontinuous. She contends that *homosociality* ('social bonds between persons of the same sex') among women, by contrast, are extensive and relatively continuous, ranging from the mother–daughter relationship through other kinds of relationship and friendship to the partnership of lesbian lovers (Sedgwick, 1985:1–5). Because male homosocial relationships are disrupted and shot through with suspicion of, rivalry with and supervision by other men, many men, fearful of confiding in and trusting their male fellows, turn to women to contribute the emotional component in their lives. This has several effects, for women as well as men. In the first instance, men often demand the emotional support of women and become angry (and even violent) when the woman in question is unable or refuses to give it. Domestic violence may be seen to spring from this situation, whether because the woman has been too preoccupied, busy or tired to respond to her man's demand for attention and support, or because she has decided, for whatever reasons, to withhold these from him or, indeed, because she has not understood the 'contract' of her relationship with him to require her to offer him attention and support, no matter what her own situation might be. The stereotypical argument from a man about why his (female) partner doesn't have dinner ready when he comes home, how it's the least she could do, considering how he kills himself working to provide a decent roof over her head, etc., etc.—we have read this scene in a hundred books, seen it in a hundred movies and watched it appear in dozens of jokes—often stems from the man's need to feel cocooned in love and support which protects him from the predatory and damaging tactics of the male world.

In the second instance, this reliance on women and their nurture contradicts the requirement made of men by the dominant model of masculinity that they be independent and emotionally self-contained. Thus some men may become violent toward their female partners because they both need the support of these women, yet fear that in acknowledging that need they allow themselves to be feminised (or emasculated) by the women. And here, of course, the woman in question may not perceive or understand that one demand of the man may conflict with other—often tacit—dynamics. These contradictory directives—one emerging from inner need, the other from external pressure—frequently lead to male confusion about the validity and consequences of emotion and of emotional need. For some men, it may lead to a grim stoicism that attempts to shut out emotion altogether; for others, it may induce a push-pull dynamic with the women in their lives, so that they demand emotional comfort and support from those women yet at the same time reject and abuse them. A comparatively small number, it would seem, actually come to terms with their confusion, sort out their needs and emotions and enjoy relationships which function much better than those of their fellow men.

There are also types of male–male friendships, like the phenomenon of mateship in Australia, which offer havens of refuge from the otherwise highly rivalrous nature of men's relation with other men. But here, too, a certain competitiveness is often inevitable, as such friends attempt to outdo one another in drinking, sexual exploits, fast living and the like. Extremely important in such male–male friendships, however, is behaviour which signals close friendship without sexual involvement, for otherwise such friends would incur the penalties meted out to homosexuals in our culture. Expressions of love and affection between men are therefore usually muted: 'He's my best mate' is often the closest many men come to saying 'I love him'. More often, though, nothing is said explicitly and the expression of affection is re-routed through activities done together—drinking, watching sports, fishing, viewing television—so that the activity itself substitutes for any articulation of love. (See Ponch Hawkes's photographic essay [1990] for some revealing comments of this nature by pairs of 'best mates'.)

The condition of many men, therefore, is lonely, traversed by tension, conflict and confusion. Like the Duke in Bartók's opera, men want love, despite the years of conditioning which teach them to suspect emotion and to flee from it. And they need love and support from other men as well as from women. The first man from whom they require love is generally their father; but, given the imperatives of masculinity issued to men in the culture, and the resultant emotionally dysfunctional nature of many men, fathers frequently fail to meet their sons' need. They may not know how to respond; they may refuse to respond; they may see their sons as rivals for the attention and love of their partners; or they may be intent on 'making men' of their sons, a goal which often excludes tenderness, physical closeness and the overt expression of affection as 'soft' and 'sissifying'. Fathers can also be distant with sons, or even largely absent from them. Unsurprisingly, therefore, many psychological case studies of men as well as confessional and autobiographical writing by men repeatedly foreground the grief and sense of loss and/or betrayal caused by their sense of alienation from their fathers: 'My father never loved me', 'My father never told me he loved me' are persistent keynotes in such texts. And such grief can lead to a diffuse anger that is often also confused, because those men want restitution, which can be difficult, if not, indeed, impossible, and find it hard to let go of unfortunate father–son relations. Often they also want revenge on their fathers, something against which the culture imposes severe sanctions but which, through the dynamic of male rivalry, it also subtly encourages.

Such needs, however, run counter to the requirement of patriarchal masculinity that men be independent and emotionally invulnerable, whence results still further confusion. Nor does such confusion assist in men's relations with women, emotional involvement with whom can be interpreted by many men as a sorry series of rejections and betrayals (this is part of the Freudian argument, that the mother disengages from the son and thus effectively hands him over to the father). Men may also perceive such relations as attempts to 'feminise' them (by demanding the expression of emotion, or of activities not deemed 'manly' in terms of masculine discourse). The whole area of emotion and feeling thus becomes a minefield for many men, often leading to the denial or repression of emotion, while at the same time enabling it to be displaced so that it may be articulated in other, less intimate or positive ways. Accordingly, anger and aggression frequently come to signify appropriate 'manly' feelings. Likewise, men may tend to substitute power relations for positive emotional ones, thus producing a confusion of love (and the need for love) with sex and sexual desire. This in turn becomes the articulation of the desire for power—over women, through the act of sexual intercourse itself, and over men, through the establishment of a reputation as a hypersexed, inexhaustible and, above all, successful 'stud'.

A further effect of the conflicting demands imposed by the patriarchal discourse of masculinity on men is the fragmentation of identity, symbolised in *Duke Bluebeard's Castle* by the seven secret chambers. We may identify these as figuring both male social identity as powerful, aggressive and rivalrous, and personal, emotional need and response. In the opera, the latter are revelations at first withheld from Judith and then, as she effects their exposure, gladly offered to her; for Bluebeard again and again expresses relief and delight and offers his thanks to Judith for exposing these obscure, secret needs and fears to the light of day (she desires to bring light into the castle to chase away its darkness).

The first, second, third and fifth chambers contain aspects of male power: the Duke's torture chamber, his armoury, his treasury and a panorama of his territories. All are either crusted over or stained by blood, or else suffused in a blood-red light. At one level, of course, this suggests that the Duke possesses sinister qualities or has engaged in sinister activities, and such symbolism is thus tied to the traditional view of Bluebeard as a wife-murderer. However, because the castle is a metaphor for the Duke himself, we may also interpret the presence of blood as suggesting that violence suffuses male identity—whether the violence is committed upon others (in the torture chamber or through the arms kept in the armoury) or upon the self (the walls of the torture chamber ooze blood, which prompts Judith to exclaim that the castle itself is bleeding). And if upon the self, the violence may have been inflicted by others in the routine way of male–male interaction, or it may have been self-administered through denial, self-deprivation or the stoic endurance of pain conventionally expected of men. The element of blood in each of these chambers suggests very strongly that the price of power is violence toward both others and oneself.

Blood also contaminates the garden that Judith finds behind the fourth door: when she asks, 'Who has bled upon your garden?', Bluebeard replies, 'Do not ask what is forbidden'. We are entitled to ask why the garden is secret: it is, after all, hidden behind a locked door. One response is that the garden represents another fragmented aspect of Bluebeard's identity as a man, namely a love of nature and of beauty that has been repressed lest it identify the man as less than manly. In this sense the question that Judith asks is forbidden because that love has been nurtured at the cost, again, of violence, whether in defending oneself against the jeers and onslaught of other men or in forcing oneself to distort one's natural love of beauty so that it becomes hidden, a secret not to be exposed to others, especially men.

Another possible response is that the Duke's hidden garden symbolises the lost Garden of Eden, and thus points to a loss of innocence. This is a form of violence in itself which, in the context of the discourse of masculinity, often occurs in the presence of violent acts—boys fighting, for example, in order to create or maintain a hierarchy that is modelled on the grand patriarchal order; or a man's coercing a woman sexually, whether by word or deed, in order to satisfy his own sexual desire or to demonstrate to others as well as to himself his status as a functioning, sexual male. In *Duke Bluebeard's Castle* the garden may thus be understood as representing innocence, fragile but already tainted with blood or violence.

Behind the sixth door Judith finds an expanse of dead, grey waters, which Bluebeard confesses are his tears. Here, again, we find another aspect of human existence and emotion held captive and secret. Big boys, as we know, don't cry; but if they do, it must be done in private, for to display personal grief and sorrow publicly is to invite the censure of other males. Thus, for example, when Bob Hawke, the former Prime Minister of Australia, wept on camera on several occasions, comments by Australians varied from approving statements about men being finally able to express emotion openly (a congratulatory response that was perhaps a little premature, given most men's refusal to engage in such public displays of emotion) to remarks about Mr Hawke being a wimp and how degrading it was to see a man cry In the same class as the latter view was the opinion that it was a 'wank' (an act of masturbation and hence not 'real' sex, an arguable proposition in itself) designed as a publicity stunt to gain the sympathy of the electorate. It is worth noting that men have not always been forbidden to express tears and other emotions publicly: the cult of sentimentalism in the eighteenth century, for instance, gave men carte blanche to demonstrate the range of their emotions.

Stiff-upper-lippery is thus not the prerogative only of Englishmen: all men are supposed to be stoic, and to bear misfortune with dignity and reserve. This unstated rule seems to be abrogated in cases of extreme catastrophe, as when on television we are shown men weeping over loved ones killed through natural disaster or war. Often, however, the typical response is to locate the emotionalism in some quality such as ethnicity: these men cry because they are Latins, say, and everyone knows how emotional and uncontrolled *they* get.

The contents of the seventh chamber come as a surprise to Judith and probably also to an audience familiar with the traditional fairy tale about Bluebeard, in which the chamber forbidden the young wife contains the corpses (in some versions, dismembered) of Bluebeard's former wives. Certainly, the earlier references to blood, as well as the concealed torture chamber, invite us to assume the worst about Judith's predecessors; and this in turn creates a sort of pornography of violence. This idea is given expression in Angela Carter's version of the story, 'The Bloody Chamber', in which the corpses of the former wives are kept on grisly and sadistic display (Carter, 1981). However, these women, as we know, are alive but kept as living mementoes of Bluebeard's past emotional life, for one is the wife of his morning, another of his midday, and the third of his evening. Now Judith, the most beloved of all, is to join them as the wife of his night.

The evidently preferred meaning of this passage of the narrative is that the Duke has failed to sustain an enduring relationship with any of these women (we might note, however, that he has nevertheless contrived to possess all of them on a continuous and permanent basis). If we take Judith as the key example, we might conclude that the failure occurred because all were over-curious about their husband's inner life and identity, and pushed too far to find out about these. We can understand this passage of the opera differently, however, by focusing on the Duke's castle as symbolic of the male body.

Woman's body is in general culturally constructed as open to men, potentially anyway, and in that openness both vulnerable and incomplete. This is why it is not 'ladylike' for a woman to sit with her legs apart: it draws attention to her openness and vulnerability to men and hence suggests her availability to them. Moreover, woman's body is seen as only weakly defining the boundary between inside and outside: men may pass through her body sexually from the outside, infants and menstrual blood and matter from the inside. Man's body, by contrast, is understood as closed and thus more complete than woman's body.

The completeness and integrity or otherwise of the body is encoded in the culture's notions of the ideal male and female physiques. While popular views of women's physiques have undergone some revision in recent years with the advent of women's weightlifting and bodybuilding programmes and competitions, there is still a general sense that women ought to look, feel and be rounder and softer than men, and hence more pliable and open—to the world in general as well as to men. Men's bodies, by contrast, should be hard, sharply defined and powerful, suggesting autonomy and self-sufficiency. Indeed, Antony Easthope uses the metaphor of the citadel or fortified 'castle of the self' to describe the way that men are conditioned to see their bodies as the boundary between the inside (largely unknown and possibly dangerous because of unsubjugated emotions or sexual inclinations) and the outside, seen as potentially invasive of the integral body. Weaknesses or gaps in the bodily surface must be repaired and vigilantly patrolled in order to prevent the outside and the inside from merging and overpowering the man's sense of himself as an autonomous entity (Easthope, 1986:35–44). Easthope's metaphor and Bartók's are thus congruent in interesting ways.

The assumed completeness and self-sufficiency of the male body is further valorised in the semiotic system of patriarchal masculinity. Woman's incompleteness disempowers her, man's completeness empowers him; she becomes inferior, he superior. Sexual penetration thus carries meanings of power as well as erotic pleasure, and the metaphors of sexual intercourse in colloquial speech, literature and pornography generally indicate this, for example in such phrases as man's 'entering' a woman and 'possessing' her. Even the biblical euphemism 'to know' a woman (carnally) implies a relationship of power gained through knowledge. Women do not generally 'know' men the same way in biblical accounts of sexuality. Such metaphors are of course prejudicial to women since they lead logically to the belief that sex is simply the penetration of another person, seen as a compliant body. Much pornography both verbal and visual thus focuses on the vulnerability (openness) of the female body to both the male gaze and the penis. Rape of women may thus be understood as an enforced/imposed openness of the female body to the male, with the act of coercion or imposition adding an erotic excitement to the event by making reality tally with ideology, namely, that *this* woman's body should be open and available to this man, just as all women's bodies should be to all men.

'Real' sex thus means the invasion by a man of another person's body, whether by invitation or force; and it is usually confirmed by the pleasure experienced *by the man*. Though in recent years men have been urged to concern themselves also with women's pleasure, this has frequently met with resistance, confusion, guilt or impatience, usually because men simply do not know much about or understand women's pleasure. As boys they learn readily enough about their own sexual pleasure through masturbation and through locker-room gossip which, as often as not, stresses the male's success in 'scoring' and in 'coming'. Frequency of sexual intercourse often counts for more than duration. And though this has a physiological basis (adolescent boys' sexual responses are generally more immediate and their sex drives higher than later in life), it is understood as a sign of the individual boy's virility, which implies power over women but also over men. In the hierarchy imposed by the dominant model of masculinity, the sexually active man ranks higher than the inactive one. For young males, then, sex becomes competitive and a means to power through achievement, as metaphors commonly used in this discourse indicate—'scoring', 'reaching first base', 'going all the way', and the like.

An adolescent male's awareness of his sexuality and of his 'conquests' can often be expressed by a sort of strut which simultaneously advertises his functioning as a sexual being and his power over peers who are either less sexually active or more modest about it. Older males may also display such behaviour, but their sexual awareness and the accompanying sense of power are often mediated, for instance, through objects like sports cars or through empowering social behaviour, such as knowing influential people or dealing in large financial transactions. That such a strut is often to be noticed also in places like gay bars among men of a wide range of ages indicates that both heterosexual and homosexual youths absorb the same sex-power codings, and that the culture of this group and of such places may encourage a sort of adolescent sexual hyperactivity.

Prohibited, however, from even being thought of in the dominant (and therefore heterosexual) discourse of masculinity is the idea that the male body too can be erotically or sexually penetrated. For if it can, what is the material difference between men's bodies and women's (setting aside, of course, genital formation and the ability to conceive and bear young)? Even penetration which can be read symbolically as erotic or sexual is likely to create unease. Thus art showing the male body transfixed by objects like lances or swords generally represent the body as dead or dying, for this is the punishment for such penetration. The many medieval and Renaissance paintings showing the martyrdom of Saint Sebastian, his body penetrated by arrows, are often unsettlingly ambiguous since they often combine the punishment with pleasure, showing the saint in a paroxysm which might be a death throe but might also be an orgasm.

If the Duke's castle in Bartók's opera is indeed symbolic of his body, Judith's importunate demands that he yield the keys to the various chambers may be understood as in effect a penetration of that body; and if so, then it is a penetration which at once feminises the Duke and masculinises Judith. The various keys which he surrenders to her may be read as phallic symbols by means of which she penetrates into one secret chamber after another, opening the Duke's body in almost a sexual way. Such a situation is simply anathema to the discourse of masculinity since it violates two cardinal requirements, namely, that the male body remain inviolate and that the female body remain passive. Judith, as woman, thus represents an extreme danger to the Duke, as man. He deals with her finally by immobilising her and relegating her to his memory of his other women.

Another way of reading this section is to see the wives as representing the sort of scorecard that many men keep of their sexual conquests. Establishing and maintaining the dynamics of a satisfying relationship are subordinated to the business of asserting one's virility (literally, in etymological terms, one's manliness) through abundant and frequent sexual activity. Often this involves disclosing to other men the state of one's sex life if it says something positive about one's desirability to women and one's technique as a seducer. This is illustrated by a Jules Feiffer cartoon, described by Harry Brod:

> We see two men talking over drinks, with one announcing to the other that he's 'quit going out'. Perplexed and disturbed, the other asks why. The first proceeds to tell a tale of the 'loveliest, purest experience I ever hope to have—a fantasy come true—me

with the most beautiful, delightful girl in the world—and she *loves* me! She loves *me!*' The story includes superb food, conversation, lovemaking, etc. The punch line has the lucky fellow telling his companion, 'And all that time do you know what I was thinking? . . . Wait till I tell the fellas'. (1990:192–3)

The Duke's wives may also represent a pornography of sex in that they are kept private, to be looked at by their husband only, just as pornographic fiction, photography and video are intended for private consumption (even if consumed by more than one person at the same time, as may be the case with video pornography). The object of desire in these sorts of text is always compliant with the viewer/voyeur's wish to see, to know carnally, as it were, through the eye. Hence woman's body is offered up to the viewer passively; and in visual pornography the viewer's gaze frequently penetrates the woman's body 'sexually' by means of what is known in the trade as the 'split beaver shot', that is, a view of the vagina fully exposed between widespread legs.

A number of feminist critics, for example, Andrea Dworkin (1989; but see also Day and Bloom, 1988; Williams, 1990; Segal and McIntosh, 1992; and Buchbinder, 1991), have argued that pornography conceptually and visually dismembers the female body in order to make it available to the male viewer's gaze and that this commits violence on the female body. Though this position on pornography may seem to some a bit excessive, *Duke Bluebeard's Castle* certainly suggests that the chamber of the wives functions as a sort of pornographic site, however tinged with sadness, nostalgia and memory, for the Duke, who relegates Judith to the function of an object once of love and desire, now simply an object.

At the beginning of the opera, Judith answers her husband's question, 'Judith, what led you to come here?', thus:

That the stone be done with weeping,
That the air once more be live,
That the walls be warm, I came here
That my lips may dry them, and my
Body warm them: Let me, Bluebeard!
Let me, husband!
Let the joyous light completely

Flood the darkness from your castle,
Let the breeze in! Let the sun in!
Soon, O soon
The air itself will ring with blessings!

Sombrely, Bluebeard replies, 'Nothing will enlight my castle'. If our reading of *Duke Bluebeard's Castle* as an allegory of masculinity is valid, this suggests the powerful resistance within most men to any change in the dominant model of masculinity which they have assimilated. To allow Judith to flood the castle with light means having to look at the castle's mysterious chambers, acknowledge their contents and own them publicly. At the end, however, the Duke remains in darkness which slowly obliterates him from view, a grim lesson to men.

3

'Well, nobody's perfect': Marginal Masculinities

In the preceding chapter we saw how a text can be read from the perspective of gender construction and politics. The preferred reading of *Duke Bluebeard's Castle* already contains these elements in the conflict between the Duke's sense of privacy and Judith's desire to penetrate to the heart of his mystery. This reading, however, repeats familiar ideas about woman's insatiable curiosity and its disastrous effect on man and on marriage. Reading in order to discover what the text has to say about the construction of masculinity itself, by contrast, exposes both the fragmentations of identity which the cultural discourse of masculinity imposes upon men and the defensiveness of many men concerning their inner, vulnerable selves. The opera, that is, not only deals with the ruined union of a particular man and his wife but also, given the text's highly symbolic nature, suggests ideas regarding the ruinous nature of masculinity, its effect on men as well as women, and the fragmentations and paralyses that it induces.

Reading a text in order to understand the gender dynamics operating within it requires us, then, to read against the grain, as it were, to look between the lines of the preferred or obvious meaning of the text. Texts articulate dominant ideologies, if only to attack or question them. However, even those texts which advance apparently subversive or challenging meanings can sometimes be deconstructed to expose a more conservative substratum of meaning. For instance, the movie *Tootsie* (1982) was much publicised upon its release as daring and innovative because it showed the central male character, Michael Dorsey (Dustin Hoffman), dressing up as a woman, 'Dorothy Michaels', and deceiving all as 'she' becomes the star of a soap opera. Overtly, the character, formerly as chauvinist and sexist a man as one could hope to meet, learns about women's oppression and finds that his consciousness has been raised.

This, then, is the film's preferred reading, a politically correct one, since it apparently both acknowledges the claims of feminism and depicts a man accepting these. One might also read the film as showing that men can be better women than actual women are. This idea is suggested when Michael's protégée and prospective girl-friend, Sandy (Terri Garr), auditions earlier for the same part in the soap opera and is rejected. It is paralleled and further reinforced by pre-release publicity anecdotes about Hoffman, still in costume and character but off the set of the film, fooling people about his identity and gender. When 'Dorothy' discovers feminism and practises it on the set of the soap opera, 'she' raises the consciousness of the crew and actors generally, and specifically liberates Julie—the real love interest (played by Jessica Lange)—from a damaging, self-denigrating relationship with the soap opera's chauvinist playboy director. The film thus also covertly suggests that men can make better feminists than women.

Such an interpretation, which exposes the film as less positive and politically correct than its preferred reading suggests, deconstructs an ostensibly feminist film to show that many of the old gender codes and requirements remain firmly in place, no matter how apparently innovative or subversive the surface narrative of the text. This reading thus also locates the film within the discourses of gender politics and conflict. However, as with Bartók's opera, it is possible to read *Tootsie* in order to find out what it has to say *to* men *about* men, about the construction of masculinity, about men's anxieties and secrets. And from this perspective we find that the film touches on two highly sensitive topics which the dominant model of masculinity often finds confronting and which offer alternatives that patriarchal masculinity finds unacceptable. These are the practice of cross-dressing and the question of homosexuality.

We should note, in discussing the phenomenon of cross-dressing, a distinction between the kind of female impersonation accomplished through *cross-dressing*—'drag', in the parlance of gay culture—and the kind achieved through *transvestism*. We can think of cross-dressing or drag as a performance. As such, it must be presented in a way that draws attention to the fact of simulation, of acting. Thus, however good the impersonation, there is often a gap or rupture in the surface that allows us to glimpse the real sex of the person through the signs, gestures and behaviour intended to convince us of the other gender. For instance, radical or gender-fuck drag, which we considered in Chapter 1, makes it very clear that the signs of clothing indicating femaleness do not correspond with the actual sex of the wearers. Drag acts in gay bars and nightclubs, moreover, attract audiences precisely because it is known that the singers and dancers are in fact male. And in nightclubs featuring female impersonators for a largely hetero-sexual audience, the point of the performance is to fool the audience into believing the performer to be female. Often, in such cabaret numbers, the performance ends with the impersonator revealing his true sex, either by speaking in a deep male voice or by removing his wig. An important element frequently to be found in cross-dressing or drag is the caricature of femininity, for instance through exaggeration of costume, gesture or gait; and such carica-ture can be at base misogynistic, inflecting the impersonation to suggest the comic or ridiculous feminine, as seen from the safety and 'normality' of the masculine.

Transvestism differs significantly from drag or cross-dressing in that the impersonator generally does not wish his impersonation to be discovered. That is, he wishes to be taken for and treated as a woman. Such performances are often carried out not on the stage but on the street, in the shops, even in the home. For some who thus impersonate women, the logical conclusion of transvestism is *transsexualism*, involving a series of operations and hormone therapies to create physically and permanently out of the person of one sex someone of the opposite sex. However, for many transves-tites cross-dressing as a woman satisfies a need to look like or feel like or be treated as a woman, without any additional desire to change sex physically. Many are married men whose wives may know of their husbands' proclivities and offer support, say, by shopping for women's clothes with (or for) them, and helping them dress and make up.

An important point here, then, is that female impersonation does not of itself imply homosexuality on the part of the impersonator. Of course, many such performers *are* gay; but then so are many policemen, bank executives, lumberjacks, teachers, lawyers and builders' labourers, 'types' usually assumed to be heterosexual. Moreover, not all gays are female impersonators or, indeed, effeminate in manner—in fact, many gay men neither approve nor enjoy female impersonation or effeminacy. We should not draw conclusions, therefore, about the sexual orientation of a man from the mere fact that he cross-dresses.

Ambivalence seems frequently to be men's response toward male-to-female cross-dressing. At one level, many men appear to be amused or even fascinated by the phenomenon of male-to-female cross-dressing—at any rate, many do not, upon being required to attend a party or gala in fancy dress, exercise much ingenuity beyond dressing up as women. This certainly seemed to be a feature in Australian culture in the 1970s; nor has it died the death, if the drag performances at a benefit by members of the Western Australian West Coast Eagles football team in 1992 are any sort of evidence. Such a disguise, moreover, may also, through the parody of femininity, feed misogynistic tendencies among men.

Many other men, however, register contempt, anxiety, unease, or even anger in the presence of other, cross-dressed men. It is, perhaps, too simple to say that the reason for this is that male-to-female cross-dressing attracts the charge of homosexuality: we have already seen, in the first place, that not all cross-dressers are gay. Moreover, why should an individual man care about or be affected by another man's dressing up as a woman? There appears to be, in some men's reception of another man's impersonation of femininity, a critical point at which tolerance or contempt crosses over into anxiety or anger. It may have to do with how the impersonation is perceived by the onlooker; that is, if it is seen as a comedy routine or an openly parodic and/or misogynistic portrayal of women, the performance may be tolerated better than if it is understood to be the actual preference or habitual practice of the cross-dressed man. In the latter case, he would be perceived by other men to have abdicated from even the gestural signs of masculinity indicated by clothing, and thus to have betrayed masculinity itself.

In *Tootsie*, Hoffman's performance, both on and off screen, suggests that gender, in addition to constituting a *semiotic* system through signs of dress, gesture, voice and so on, may also be a *rhetorical* system. Rhetoric, the classical art of persuasion, is usually limited conceptually to speech and writing, that is, the verbal arts. But *Tootsie* invites us to suppose that if the signs of gender are artfully enough arranged, they cease to indicate a gender identity founded on real sexual difference, becoming instead a system designed to persuade the viewer of the presence of a particular gender identity, regardless of the real sex of the person so indicated. This is, of course, the art of the professional or habitual female impersonator. However, we may say that if we read *Tootsie* thus, the film disturbingly suggests that the signs of gender identity can be entirely self-referential (that is, not referring outside them-selves to any actual sexual identity) and hence, in an important way, fictitious.

Such an insight of course puts into question common social assumptions that gender behaviour and sexual difference are not only tied together naturally but are fixed in the way they refer to one another. So, one might argue, in a culture which denies masculinity to gay men it is possible for gays to produce the rhetorical signs of heterosexual masculinity and thus to 'impersonate' the appropriate, acceptable identity. This line of thinking leads interestingly to the further idea that perhaps the dominant gender identity of hetero-sexual masculinity is itself an impersonation learned by all men in the culture (a suggestion we encountered in Chapter 1, in the notion of 'coming out of the closet'). Such a reading of *Tootsie* proposes that the distinction between masculine and feminine may be more blurred than we as a culture might generally want to believe, so that the shift from the one to the other may in fact be easier and more frequently made than we might think.

That shift becomes troublesome to a culture which functions through (and thus needs) strongly defined binaries, such as male/female, masculine/feminine, man/woman, and heterosexual/ho-mosexual. Intermediate terms, such as 'hermaphrodite' (an indi-vidual born with both male and female primary sexual characteristics) or 'bisexual' (an individual sexually attracted to both male and female) create anomalies. Apart from ignoring them entirely, the culture generally deals with such identities or behaviours by first defining them as abnormal (that is, against nature) or deviant (that is, wilfully selected by the individual concerned), and then by institutionalising affected individuals, whether in various sorts of hospitals (for observation, 'cure' or ongoing treatment) or in prisons (in order to punish them for contravening God's law, man's law or both).

The unease that many experience in the presence of cross-dressed individuals, then, may be traced to their sense of the blurring or erasure of the otherwise clear lines defining and separating male from female, masculine from feminine. With the disintegration of such boundaries, the individual's sense of how the social world is constituted is threatened: former, apparently self-evident 'truths' are contradicted, and other possibilities (many remaining only provisional or conditional, and hence still uncertain) offered. With their world-view thus menaced, it is not surprising that some men react angrily to the mere fact of a cross-dressed male.

The Russian theorist Mikhail Bakhtin (1984) suggests that where such official laws, definitions and prohibitions exist, there is also always the possibility of their being ignored, flouted or breached. This is analogous to the notion of the resistant discourse, discussed earlier; but Bakhtin argues in addition that such contravention may be permitted during agreed (or conceded) periods by the official authorities, and that it operates as a sort of safety valve to allow high feeling and other sorts of 'steam' to escape. This Bakhtin calls *carnival*, and he proposes that the carnivalesque is also the home of the grotesque, where otherwise antithetical properties or characteristics are matched together in the same being: beast with human, youth with age, male with female, and so on (Bakhtin, 1984:196–277 and 303–67). Thus animal masks are a frequent feature of much carnival semiotic, as are representations of ambivalent sexual identity. Think, too, of the bearded lady and the half-man, half-woman—apparent freaks who indeed might once have been exhibited at circuses, fairs and carnivals, but who have long since become semiotic signs themselves of the carnival grotesque, so that the mere mention or appearance of one of these is sufficient to signify both carnival and the grotesque.

Cross-dressing (male-to-female or female-to-male) can thus be regarded as carnivalesque in nature and thence as potentially liberating, breaching, if only temporarily, dominant codes and discourses of gender. Hence its appropriateness in confronting certain assumptions about gender, as when women dress in mannish clothes in order to challenge men and their notions of what constitutes the feminine; and when men choose to wear women's apparel, whether because they wish to challenge dominant models of masculinity, or because they like the feel of such clothing, or because they want to surprise passers-by or paying audiences. The other kind of response to cross-dressing, then—amusement, participation or other positive involvement with cross-dressing as an activity—would seem to derive from the sense of liberation and of openly flouting the restrictive, defining codes of thought, attitude and behaviour pertaining to gender.

We should remember that Bakhtin regards the carnivalesque as a feature essentially of late medieval European culture which has been replaced by rather less robust or challenging forms of festival since the Renaissance. However, an event like the annual Sydney Gay and Lesbian Mardi Gras (one of the largest celebrations of male and female homosexuality in the world) might serve as an interesting contemporary instance of carnival since it includes an officially permitted street parade in which gender identity is consciously made ambiguous through often flamboyant cross-dressing by many of the participants and their flaunting of non-conformist sexuality, both as a political statement about the widespread oppression of gay women and men, and as a comment on conventional attitudes. Moreover, that many heterosexual people arrive in crowds to witness the Mardi Gras parade and to participate in the party that follows suggests that they, too, see the event as carnival, a moment when conventional behaviours and attitudes may be relaxed and the unconventional enjoyed.

Cross-dressing, however, is always only a temporary challenge: after all, when the clothes of the other sex are doffed, the true sex of the wearer is inevitably revealed. The confusions that cross-dressing can induce in people are thus likewise of a temporary nature: after the moment of amusement, contempt or anger has passed, the onlooker can return to the safety of his or her assumptions about sex and gender. A much more threatening challenge, and a permanent one, is the one offered by a non-normative sexual orientation and practice; and homosexuality offers such a challenge to dominant notions of masculinity.

Implicit in what we have said so far is the idea that the dominant discourse of masculinity in our culture defines it first as heterosexual. This is made explicit, of course, by the presence of homophobic attitudes, behaviours and laws in various western societies. The word 'homophobia' was coined in the 1920s, according to Sara Tulloch in *The Oxford Dictionary of New Words*, when it signified 'fear or dislike of men', through the combination of the Latin *homo* ('man') with the Greek *-phobia* ('fear'). It did not gain currency, however, until the late 1960s, when the word underwent a transformation of meaning by aligning 'homo' with 'homosexual', so that it signified 'fear or dislike of homosexuals'. George Weinberg is credited by some with reinventing the word with its new signification (for instance, by Segal, 1990:158), but *The Oxford Dictionary of New Words* is of the opinion that he merely popularised the word in his writing during the 1970s, though the term 'did not reach a wide audience until the advent of Aids [*sic*] turned the phenomenon it described into a growing reality' (Tulloch, 1991). Weinberg, however, used 'homophobia' more precisely to denote 'the dread of being in close quarters with homosexuals' (Weinberg, 1975:4), suggesting a psychological condition akin, say, to arachnophobia, the (irrational) fear of being close to spiders. Later, it came more broadly to mean 'an irrational fear of homosexuals'. John Boswell argues that this is inaccurate and that etymologically the term actually means 'an irrational fear of the same', an interesting idea in the light of what we have said above regarding men's competitiveness with, and hence fear of, one another (Boswell, 1980:46, note 11). The confusions arise because 'homo-' in 'homosexual' derives etymologically from the Greek *homos*, meaning 'same,' and signifies sexual attraction to those of the same sex, just as 'heterosexual' signifies sexual attraction to those of the opposite sex (the Greek *heteros* means 'other'). However, because the prefix 'homo-' may be derived from either the Greek or the Latin, muddles of meaning are perhaps inevitable. Thus, 'homophobia' may be commonly understood to refer specifically to a fear of and a hostility toward male homosexuals only.

At any rate, 'homophobia' now generally refers also to the acts of hostility and aggression toward (usually male) homosexuals occasioned by the revulsion from or dislike toward the very notion or fact of (male) homosexuality. That the mere existence of homosexuality and of men who practise it can excite extreme repugnance, outrage, fury and violence in other men who are presumably not directly affected by it suggests that homosexuality offers a threat to a masculinity that wants discursively to see itself as seamlessly, unassailably heterosexual.

Media images reinforce this. There are few positive images of homosexual men to be found in the newspapers or on television: traditionally, such men have either been defined as comic and hence politically impotent figures; or they have been seen as deviants staining and destroying the social and moral fabric of the world we live in, a fit subject for sensationalist reporting. The latter image has been strongly foregrounded during the decade since the discovery of AIDS through its labelling as a 'gay disease', calls to quarantine gay men and/or those with HIV/AIDS, and the heightening of homophobia, both formally, through political or legal vilification and moralising, and informally, through violence offered on the street to men known or assumed to be gay. In other words, homosexuality as a practice of *some* men in the culture is unacceptable as a feature of masculinity as a whole.

Yet homosexual men do not arrive out of nowhere: they are our fathers, brothers, friends, colleagues, even, indeed, ourselves. They are mostly born into and brought up in 'normal' (that is, non-homosexual or 'straight') households and learn the same codes pertaining to gender behaviour and masculine sexuality as all other males in the society. Why, then, do fathers, brothers, friends, colleagues and we ourselves often react negatively, often violently, to the discovery that one or another male of our acquaintance happens to prefer other men as sexual, emotional and domestic partners? Indeed, so intense can be this response, and the social consequences so punitive, that many men who discover such inclinations in themselves attempt to stifle or 'cure' them in some fashion.

We have already seen that not all societies universally reject homosexuality. Indeed, some have actually integrated the phenomenon as part of the cultural make-up of the people. Thus, in classical Greece, homosexual relations between adolescent boys and older men were regarded as part of the former's induction into the culture and politics of particular states like Athens or Sparta, and as part of the latter's educational and civic duty toward the younger male generation which would eventually lead the state. We should beware, however, of idealising or romanticising this cultural and sexual phenomenon as 'Greek love', which many nineteenth- and early twentieth-century homosexual men were prone to do; and we should be careful, too, about assuming that male–male sexual relations in classical Greek society paralleled those in our own (see Dover, 1989; Halperin, 1990). Other non-European societies have also regarded homosexual relations as integral to the process by which young males reach adulthood (see Greenberg, 1988; Rubin, 1993).

In western (that is, Judaeo-Christian) societies the phenomenon of male homosexuality has been seen as a moral choice made by the individual. Sodomy, the term by which the practice was known until the last century, was thus a sin, which the individual might repent. During the nineteenth century, however, homosexuality came to be viewed through the lens of a medical discourse which transformed a sexual *practice* into a sexual *pathology* (see Foucault, 1980, 1987; Davidson, 1987).

The term 'homosexuality' was devised by Károly Mária Benkert, a Hungarian physician, in 1869 as part of a response to this discourse of sexual pathology. Ironically, 'heterosexuality', signifying 'normal' sexual inclinations and practice, came into existence as a term *after* the invention of 'homosexuality', the departure from such normality, in order to maintain the binary distinction. Male–male sexual practice, according to this response, was divided into two categories. The first was *inversion*, which supposedly signified a biological as well as sexual malfunction innate in some men; the second was *perversion*, which signified a deliberate choice made by some men who were otherwise purportedly heterosexual.

The inversion/perversion argument was developed as a political strategy to lessen the penalties imposed upon men arrested and convicted for 'unnatural' sexual behaviour. It postulated the existence of a 'third' sex in nature which included both women (lesbians) and men (male homosexuals) who had somehow lost the thread of the 'normal' sexual narrative. So, it was argued, if individuals were discovered to be 'inverts', legal penalties should be modified since those individuals could not help themselves, being the victims of an unfortunate sport of nature. Rather, they should be helped medically, psychologically and socially to live with their infirmity. On the other hand, because 'perverts' wilfully chose to run counter to their natural sexuality they should be subjected to the full force of the law.

This attempt to explain and exonerate homosexuality, however well-intentioned, made for more confusion since, in the first place, it was—and is—not easy in fact to distinguish inversion from perversion. Second, it assumed that, whereas perverts would corrupt normal citizens in the pursuit of their erotic pleasures, inverts would be attracted only to other inverts. This, however, was by no means the case. Third, it tended to blur the lines between a non-normative sexuality as sin (the traditional view) and as medical (or psychological) condition (the more recent opinion). Finally and importantly, the devising of these categories of course implicitly accepted the medical discourse which now sought scientifically to find material causes for a troublesome phenomenon that hitherto had been ascribed to moral degeneration and sinful choice.

Homosexuality disturbs the dynamics and ideology of the dominant discourse of masculinity in our culture because, although it appears to be part of another tidy binary (heterosexuality/ homosexuality), it does not in fact align so cleanly with others, which, we might note, have to do with biological sex and implied gender and social identity, namely:

male	female
masculine	feminine
man	woman

The binary 'heterosexuality/homosexuality' does not fit properly in the above columns—we cannot add the terms of this binary thus:

heterosexual	homosexual
male	female
masculine	feminine
man	woman

Though the dominant model of masculinity certainly appropriates heterosexuality for itself, we cannot logically align 'homosexuality' exclusively with 'female/feminine/woman'. Moreover, though homosexuality is the second term of the binary, it cuts across the distinctions created by the other pairs, so that, in the case of 'male' + 'homosexual', maleness is apparently connected with and thus implies, femaleness, femininity and 'woman-ness' in men so designated. These characteristics in turn are associated with weakness, passivity and vulnerability, aspects assumed in women but not encouraged in men by the dominant model of masculinity. Yet not all male homosexuals behave in a feminine or effeminate manner, or think of themselves in those terms.

In the preceding chapter we considered how masculine discourse regards real sex as penetrative, and also how the male body is constructed as integral and inviolate. It is not surprising, therefore, that in the popular mind male homosexual activity is almost always equated with penetration, though there are other forms of sexual gratification (which have been much foregrounded and publicised as part of the safe-sex campaigns against the spread of HIV/AIDS). Penetration of a homosexual kind chiefly takes two forms, fellatio (oral sex) and anal intercourse, and in each case the recipient of his partner's penis is popularly characterised as feminine. This leads, perhaps inevitably, to the assumption that the recipient is the 'wife' or 'woman' in the relationship, something which many gay political writers reject, for two reasons. First, because such a way of conceptualising homosexual activities and relationships imposes heterosexual norms, including the notion that sexual roles are fixed (male=active, inserter of penis, female=passive, recipient of penis), whereas in reality homosexual partners may change roles, as fancy and desire dictate. Second, because it imports into same-sex relationships the inequities of patriarchal ideology, suggesting that the recipient is somehow less than masculine because he performs the 'wife's' role, as suggested by the terms 'active' and 'passive': the underlying assumption here is that 'real' men are active, that is, penetrating, while women and 'fake' men remain passive, that is, penetrated. For this reason, some theorists, clinicians and sociologists now prefer to describe the roles as those of 'inserter' (of the penis) and 'insertee', though these terms are likewise afflicted with semantic and ideological difficulties, not the least of which is the suggestion of some kind of coin-operated sexual vending machine. Another pair of terms currently gaining ascendancy is 'the insertive partner' and 'the receptive partner'. These terms also allow the individual's preferred sexual practice to be described as 'anally insertive sex(ual intercourse)' or 'anally receptive sex(ual intercourse)'.

For many men, however, such terms are unnecessary nuances of a single, irreducible fact, namely, that the male homosexual is a man who allows his body to be penetrated by another man. In this, the gay man permits that which the discourse of masculinity absolutely forbids—the disruption of the integrity and inviolability of the male body—and so challenges the authority and power of that discourse. In his betrayal of the dominant codes of masculinity, the homosexual man proposes a range of other possible codes, which in turn threaten to destabilise the discourse. The effect, inevitably, is to make men in general feel uneasy and threatened.

Another aspect of homosexuality which is dangerous to masculine discourse is the fact that, despite popular assumptions about and stereotypes of homosexuals, one cannot really 'tell' which man is gay and which is not. The behaviour of some men does indeed correspond to the stereotype; that is how stereotypes come into existence and why they work. We have already considered some reasons for stereotypical behaviour, such as the deliberate flouting of conventions, the element of carnival and so on. David Fernbach proposes, in addition, that in a binary-driven culture the only models available to gay men are those of the dominant masculinity (which by definition precludes and prohibits homosexuality) or femininity. He argues that many gay men therefore behave in a feminine manner because this is the only option available to them, given the closure to them of dominant masculinity and its hostility toward them (Fernbach, 1981:61–112).

The gay men whose behaviour (language, gestures, and so on) conform to those of cultural stereotypes of the male homosexual are of course the most noticeable to the population at large. However, mannerisms associated with 'obviously' gay men do not necessarily characterise *all* gay men; nor are all flamboyant and apparently effeminate men necessarily homosexual in their erotic inclinations. Gay and lesbian groups estimate, largely on the basis of the 1948 study which came to be known as the Kinsey Report (Kinsey et al., 1948), that male and female homosexuals constitute around 10 per cent of any population. This is, at best, only a notional figure since accurate statistics showing the percentage of the population that is homosexual are notoriously difficult to come by: respondents are understandably reluctant, given the repercussions possible in a society largely hostile to gay men, to admit to homosexuality, even

when complete confidentiality regarding such information is prom-
ised by the researcher.

Another reason why it is difficult to get an accurate fix on such
statistics is that the term 'homosexual' is made to cover a wide
variety of possible same-sex activities, in terms not only of the
specific erotics involved but also of frequency of such contact over
short periods and over the course of an individual's life. Can we, for
instance, define a man as 'homosexual' if he engaged in sexual
activity with other males during his late adolescence and early
twenties, but then married a woman, and enjoyed only heterosexual
sex thereafter? Does 'homosexual' mean that the person concerned
favours or always engages in anal sex? Is a 'homosexual' one who
is the recipient of the penis in anal sex or also the one who inserts
it? And what of the man who has known from an early age that he
is sexually drawn to other men but who has never responded to or
acted on that attraction?

The Kinsey Report indicated that as many as 37 per cent of the
male population of the United States had had a homosexual
experience to the point of orgasm. Michael Ruse proposes that if
one factors into this number various other statistics, including a
notional number of those who had had 'yearnings', the statistic
might have been as high as 50 per cent of the men who responded
to the Kinsey investigation (Ruse, 1988:4). Heather Formaini cites
figures for men who have sex with men as high as 60 to 70 per cent
of the male population (Formaini, 1990:181). Such statistics, however, must be read carefully, for a man who 'has sex with men' may
do so only once, or infrequently: this does not of itself make such
an individual a 'homosexual', a term implying a more continuous
attraction to and sexual dealing with men. In addition, Formaini's
statistics are derived from the work of clinical psychologists and
psychotherapists, and it may well be that the population of men
seeing such professionals contains a high percentage of men with
homosexual or merely homo-erotic leanings, because these are
likely to produce anxiety and neurosis in men trying to live up to
the heterosexual model of masculinity dominant in the culture.

More recent studies in the United States have suggested that
homosexual men constitute only 1 per cent of the population
(Painton, 1993:41), but these have been criticised not only for the

sample which provided the basis for their statistics but also for the nature of the survey and its questions (ibid.:42–3). Such a low percentage, moreover, has political implications for gay men: conservative Phyllis Schlafly is quoted as saying that 'it shows politicians they don't need to be worried about 1% of the population' (ibid.:41). It would seem, then, that the statistic which proposes that homosexuals constitute 10 per cent of any population may still be a reasonable estimate. But this statistic too has implications: it means that one out of every ten men we know may be gay. Yet do we actually recognise that one to be a homosexual?

One of the reasons why the announcement that the movie star Rock Hudson was suffering from AIDS was so shocking was that it was coupled with the news that he was homosexual: yet Hudson never in any of his films played an 'obvious' homosexual. This is because the 'obviousness' of homosexual behaviour depends on its corresponding with stereotypes, whereas indications are that effeminate homosexual men are in fact only a small, if easily recognisable, section of the gay population. This is probably small consolation to men who fear and repudiate homosexuality, for the homosexual man thus comes to be seen as an insidious type, a chameleon who can exist within patriarchy ostensibly as an ordinary, 'normal' (that is, heterosexual) man and yet, by the mere fact of his sexual inclinations, undermine the equation made in the dominant model of masculinity between manliness and heterosexuality.

We may summarise the issue thus: since dominant notions of masculinity assume heterosexuality to be the norm in men, homosexuality may be interpreted as a failure of masculinity. On the one hand, this has led, as we have seen, to attempts to explain homosexuality in terms of medicine—offering a range of 'causes' for that 'failure', for instance hormone deficiency, physiological malformation, and various environmental factors, such as biochemical alterations through vitamin or other nutritional deficiency—and in terms of psychology—the Freudian standby, for example, of the family constellated by a dominant mother and a weak or absent father. These, in turn, encourage the view that homosexuality is either a curable ailment ('cures' vary from hormone injections to such psychological strategies as aversion therapy) or an irreversible disease.

Alternatively, homosexuality may be interpreted as a subversion, conscious or unconscious, of 'the normal' (whatever that may be: different cultures impose different criteria of normality). This has been the traditional, moral view of homosexuality as a sin, that is, as a conscious choice which the sinner, having once made it, should also be able to unmake. This is the argument advanced by the medieval Church, that sodomy, as it was known, was *contra naturam*, against nature. To repudiate it was to return to nature and to the will of God. (See Goodich, 1979; Bray, 1982.) Modern arguments that homosexuality is against nature are, however, often grounded in rather vague notions about 'nature' which do not necessarily identify it with divine will and are also notoriously inaccurate in their observation of 'nature' (see Boswell, 1980:11–15). Same-sex sexual behaviour has been noted in various species, though the causes may not always be identical or, indeed, identifiable. The Darwinian version of the argument against homosexuality as unnatural assumes that the survival of the species depends entirely on the procreative potential of all members of the species. But Darwin's thesis actually postulated diversity among members of the species, and it may be that homosexuality represents such diversity, even if it is non procreative. This, too, is arguable: it is clear, from the account of other cultures both past and present, that homosexual behaviour does not necessarily exclude heterosexual relations. It would appear that it is the either/or distinction set up in our cultural discourse of sexuality that enables the assumption that homosexuals are non-procreative.

The idea that homosexuality may be subversive of the 'normal' also underlies popular notions of the male homosexual as seeking to 'convert' others to his own sexual preference. Setting aside the question of whether or not males can be so easily converted to homosexuality, we might note that this view perceives homosexuality as deliberately and mischievously setting out to corrupt and distort the sexual values as well as the practices of the society. This particular perception of the phenomenon of homosexuality has been exacerbated, perhaps inevitably, by the AIDS epidemic, so that the gay man is often now branded not only as attempting to corrupt society morally but also as seeking to poison it virally.

These two categories of popular response to homosexuality are frequently confused (and confusing), for they want homosexuality to be both an unfortunate accident of nature (or of environment) and a conscious programme of subversion. Furthermore, they want the gay man's sexual preference to be both unnatural (that is, running *contrary* to nature) and contagious (that is, running *according* to nature, in this case, according to the patterns of disease and infection). The cultural discourse pertaining to homosexuality seeks to embrace both categories, which is one reason why debate on the issue of homosexuality frequently ends up in irrational and prejudicial contentiousness, rather than in a clear-headed and fair-minded gathering and examination of facts.

A different way of perceiving the relationship of homosexuality to heterosexuality is to see these as parts of a single discourse, rather than as two conflicting discourses. This is what Michel Foucault argues in the first volume of his *History of Sexuality* (1980), in which he proposes that the modern category of 'the homosexual' is actually produced by a discourse of sexuality which commenced in the eighteenth century and developed further in the nineteenth. We might add that the category of the masculine is also produced discursively by a double movement, which defines the masculine first in terms of sex—male, as against female—and then in terms of sexuality—heterosexual, as against homosexual. The category of the homosexual is thus central to the definition of masculinity in our culture. Consequently, attempts to repress or eradicate homosexuality (whether as activity or merely as concept) are doomed to fail, unless the related category of the masculine—as we presently understand it, and which the category of the homosexual helps to define—is also to be done away with.

Nevertheless, the simple existence of male homosexuality, as we have observed, apparently issues a challenge to dominant discourses of masculinity; and society often responds by discriminating against gays, targeting them for ridicule, physical violence, and moral and legal coercion. Such a result, we might note, is akin to the patriarchal response to femininity and to feminism: these also challenge the dominant discourses of masculinity, and are frequently dealt with in similar ways.

The twin issues of cross-dressing and male homosexuality are raised in *Tootsie* through Michael's creation of 'Dorothy Michaels', and his subsequent impersonation of this fictitious woman. We might note in passing that though the name 'Dorothy' is, at the narrative level of *Tootsie*, simply an echo of 'Dorsey', it was also once a code-word in the parlance of an older generation of gay men. To ask if so-and-so was 'a friend of Dorothy' was to inquire whether he was homosexual. Jeff, Michael's flatmate, asks with mock seriousness at one point whether Michael is cross-dressing because he needs the job with the soap opera or because he really just wants to get into women's clothes. Moreover, Michael himself points out ironically that, whereas Sandy begins to think that he is gay, Julie believes him to be lesbian, while her father, Les, wants 'Dorothy' to become his wife, a confusion which turns on the multiple possibilities of homosexuality caused by the act of cross-dressing. Potentially, the premise of *Tootsie* could seriously interrogate cultural assumptions about sex, sexuality and gender, especially in the way the film constructs cross-purposes in the various romances between a man and a woman (Michael and Julie), a woman and a woman ('Dorothy' and Julie), and a man and a man (Michael and Les). The gender politics of this film are comparable with those of Shakespeare's *As You Like It*, in which the crossing of gender boundaries is intensified by the fact that in Elizabethan theatres a boy actor played the female character Rosalind who impersonates a young man who in turn impersonates a woman so that Orlando can practise his 'lines' as Rosalind's intended lover. In fact, however, *Tootsie* fails to make much of its opportunities. There is never any real question that Michael is heterosexual; and though the movie ends with Julie asking Michael whether she can borrow his yellow Halston dress, it recuperates male heterosexuality through the promise, if not the actuality, of a happy-ever-after conclusion to the Michael–'Dorothy'–Julie relationship by removing the disturbing central character and restoring normal heterosexual relations.

An earlier film about cross-dressing offers a narrative that is somewhat more disturbing to the directives and needs of the dominant model of masculinity. Billy Wilder's *Some Like It Hot*, made in 1959, seems to constitute a point of reference for *Tootsie* in that the more recent film echoes or quotes from the earlier one. In both, for instance, the act of cross-dressing is undertaken in order to secure a job; in both, the cross-dressing leads to comedy when the central characters fall in love with a woman met as a consequence of obtaining the job. But whereas *Tootsie* re-establishes normative heterosexuality at the end of the narrative, *Some Like It Hot* leaves the issue partially unresolved and thus discordant with the dominant model of masculinity.

The story begins in Chicago in 1929, during the period in the United States known as Prohibition, when an attempt was made on moral grounds to curb the production and consumption of alcohol (1920–33). That year also saw the Wall Street market crash and the beginning of the Depression, when many thousands lost their jobs and could not find any further work. Joe (Tony Curtis) and Gerry (Jack Lemmon) are musicians in a band playing in a Chicago speakeasy (a club illegally serving liquor), who lose their jobs when the place is raided by the police. In their search for work they learn that a band called Sweet Sue and Her Society Syncopators is looking for a tenor saxophone and a bass player. Though these are the instruments they play, Joe and Gerry are the wrong sex. Gerry suggests, in his desperate need to find a job and make some money, that they could impersonate female musicians; but Joe discards this, preferring instead to go for a one-night gig celebrating St Valentine's Day on a university campus. As ill luck would have it, Joe and Gerry inadvertently witness a Capone-style St Valentine's Day Massacre in a garage where they have gone to pick up a car in order to make their engagement at the university.

They escape from 'Spats' Columbo and his gang; but, as witnesses sought both by gangsters and police, and fearing for their lives, Joe and Gerry take the job with the all-woman jazz band in order to disappear for a while from the limelight, for the band is to appear at the Seminole Ritz Hotel in Miami, Florida. En route they meet Sugar Cane, née Kowalchek (Marilyn Monroe), a singer and ukelele player, to whom both Joe (now 'Josephine') and Gerry ('Daphne') are attracted. Joe has to remind his friend that he is now a girl and that he cannot make a pass at Sugar, who confides to Joe that she has a thing for tenor sax players but that they always leave her in the lurch. This, of course, interests Joe, himself a tenor sax player; but Sugar announces that her ambition in Miami is to find a millionaire, marry him and live in wealth and security for the rest of her life (this is probably an allusion to another of Monroe's comedy movies, *How to Marry a Millionaire*, made in 1953). She particularly wants to find a millionaire with glasses, since she believes that spectacles signify someone gentle whose eyes have been weakened by reading the appropriate columns in the *Wall Street Journal*.

In Miami, Gerry makes the acquaintance of Osgood Fielding III (Joe E. Brown), a millionaire who has been married seven or eight times (he cannot remember, but in any case Mama is keeping count, he tells 'Daphne'). Gerry, who becomes the object of Osgood's attentions, is appalled by the lewdness of the elderly playboy, exclaiming to Joe that he cannot understand Osgood's behaviour, since he himself isn't even pretty; to which Joe responds that such dirty old men don't care as long as the person at whom they make a pass is (or appears to be) female. He meanwhile has secretly appropriated the band manager's glasses and suitcase and, disguising himself later by resuming male costume, engineers a meeting with Sugar when she is on the beach with the rest of the girls, including 'Daphne'. He leads her to believe that he is the heir to the Shell Oil fortune and that he owns one of the luxury yachts anchored in the bay. 'Daphne', who has come up in order to protect his interest in Sugar, sees through Joe's disguise and attempts to expose his friend by racing with Sugar back to the hotel room he shares with Joe. He hopes to reach the room before Joe and thus expose the real identity of 'Shell Oil, Jr'. But Joe, who has now also appropriated a bicycle, has returned ahead of them, and, as 'Josephine', is apparently enjoying a bubble bath. We later learn that, in his haste to forestall the exposure planned by Gerry, Joe is fully clothed under the bubbles.

Joe persuades Gerry to acquiesce to the attentions of Osgood, who wants to take 'Daphne' to his yacht for a late supper after the show. Joe, with designs of his own, further persuades Gerry to tell Osgood that 'she' ('Daphne') gets seasick, and would rather spend the evening with him on land. We then watch Joe and Sugar on Osgood's yacht (conveniently vacated on Joe's prompting), where he effects his seduction of the gullible Sugar by claiming that he is impotent and that all efforts to cure him have proven useless. Sugar, who would rather marry a young millionaire than an old one and who is falling for Joe anyway, brings about a 'cure' of her own by kissing him voluptuously over and over, until Joe announces that at last he is feeling 'something'.

Meanwhile, 'Daphne' and her millionaire are tangoing the night

away to the rhythms of a Latin American band at a roadhouse.
Gerry's distaste and humiliation at having to go through this
rigmarole gradually modulate into something like enjoyment and
active participation. In the early hours of the dawn, when Joe
returns to the hotel room, he finds Gerry in a mood of inebriated
elation, shaking a pair of maracas (a souvenir, presumably, from the
band). He announces his engagement to Osgood, whereupon the
following dialogue[1] (one of the funniest in the film) ensues:

JOE: You can't marry Osgood.

GERRY: Do you think he's too old for me?

JOE: Why would a guy want to marry a guy?

GERRY: Security! . . . I'm not stupid, I know there's a
           problem: his mother! We need her approval, but
           I'm not worried, because—I—don't—smoke! [This
           alludes to an earlier conversation between
           'Daphne' and Osgood, when the latter tells 'her'
           that his mother disapproved of his last wife be-
           cause she smoked.] (*Punctuated by rattles on the
           maracas.*)

JOE: Gerry, there's another problem, like: What are you
           going to do on your honeymoon?

GERRY: We've been discussing that. He wants to go to the
           Riviera, but I kind of lean toward Niagara Falls.

JOE: Gerry, you're out of your mind! How are you
           going to get away with this?

GERRY: I don't expect it to last, Joe. I'll tell him the truth
           when the time comes.

JOE: Like when?

GERRY: Like right after the ceremony . . . Then we get a
           quick annulment, he makes a nice settlement on
           me, and I keep getting those alimony cheques
           every month. (*More rattles on the maracas.*)

However, the arrival of 'Spats' Columbo and his boys for a
convention of the Friends of Italian Opera (a cover for a meeting
of several gangs) puts paid to the plans of both Joe and Gerry. They
decide to flee but before he goes, Joe, as 'Shell Oil, Jr', breaks the
news to Sugar that he must go to Venezuela to marry for dynastic

and economic reasons. He sends Gerry's engagement gift from Osgood, a diamond bracelet, together with Gerry's orchids, another gift from Osgood, to Sugar, and the two hapless musicians attempt to make good their escape. Foiled, they end up witnessing yet another massacre, this time of 'Spats' and his men, at the behest of Little Bonaparte, the president of the Friends of Italian Opera.

Joe tells Gerry to call Osgood on his yacht and to inform him that 'Daphne' will join him; then, as 'Josephine', he goes for the last time to watch Sugar perform. He allows his disguise to slip before running out of the hotel, pursued by a posse of gangsters and police. Meanwhile, Sugar deduces the truth and runs after him, joining Joe and Gerry just as they are about to leave in Osgood's launch. She ignores all of Joe's protests about his worthlessness as a partner, and the two kiss and make up in the back of the launch. Meanwhile, in the front, Gerry decides to tell Osgood the truth when the happy millionaire announces that Mama wants 'Daphne' to wear the dress she herself was married in:

GERRY: I can't get married in your mother's dress. She and I—we are not built the same way.

OSGOOD: We can have it altered.

GERRY: Osgood, I'm going to level with you: we can't get married at all.

OSGOOD: Why not?

GERRY: Well, in the first place, I'm not a natural blonde.

OSGOOD: It doesn't matter.

GERRY: I smoke. I smoke all the time.

OSGOOD: I don't care.

GERRY: I have a terrible past. For three years now, I've been living with a saxophone player.

OSGOOD: I forgive you.

GERRY: (*tragically*): I can never have children.

OSGOOD: We can adopt some.

GERRY: You don't understand, Osgood! (*Pulling off his wig*) I'm a man!

OSGOOD: Well, nobody's perfect.

Though heterosexuality is largely maintained as the norm in *Some Like It Hot*, first through the presence of Marilyn Monroe, who as an actress was an icon of the woman desirable (and possibly accessible) to all men, and second through the romance between Joe and Sugar, the dominant model of masculinity is none the less shown to be basically unstable. That Joe should carry through his seduction of Sugar by feigning impotence touches on an issue of enormous significance and a source of great anxiety to men, namely, the ability to 'perform' sexually. Given the myth of the dominant model of masculinity—that men's sexuality is a powerful urge seeking satisfaction anywhere/everywhere, at any/every moment—impotence (the inability to rise to that sexual need) is more than a passing embarrassment for many men. Indeed, if it were only that, many men would not suffer impotence as much, since it is often brought on by what therapists call 'performance anxiety'. It constitutes, rather, a denial of the sufferer's masculinity as well as of his virility. The film's foregrounding of this is thus quite daring. But because we know that Joe is not in fact impotent, and that this is a seducer's stratagem, the anxiety of impotence is defused and turned into comedy.

Gerry, however, whose attachment to Sugar constructs him as apparently heterosexual, is given traits which align him with the cross-dressing male and the homosexual. In the earlier part of the film he evidently has no girlfriend, whereas Joe appears to be stringing several women along. Moreover, it is Gerry who first thinks up the idea of cross-dressing in order to obtain the jobs (at that point in the film the two musicians are not yet under threat from 'Spats'). Though the two agree that their names as women will be 'Geraldine' and 'Josephine', Gerry later settles on 'Daphne' because he likes the name better, suggesting that he is entering more enthusiastically than Joe into the spirit of cross-dressing and cross-gender identity. And it is Gerry who, toward the end of the film, betrays both of them in their attempt to escape from the mobsters in the hotel because he continues to wear high heels with his bell-boy's uniform.

Gerry also needs to be reminded every so often about both his sex and his gender-performance. After meeting Sugar, he is in danger of exposing the fact that both he and Joe are not in fact women, and Joe must tell him that he is supposed to be a girl, to which Gerry responds, 'I'm a girl—I wish I was dead—I'm a girl'.

Later, when he tells Joe about his engagement to Osgood, Joe reminds him that he is male, and Gerry moans, 'I'm a boy—I wish I were dead!'.

As 'Daphne', Gerry acts more outrageously in an attempt to be girlish, when, for example, he twitters to the other band members about the divine little seamstress he employs. In addition, an element of feminine spitefulness (as perceived, at least, by men) enters his behaviour. Upon arrival at the Seminole Ritz, Gerry as 'Daphne' rounds upon Joe in jealousy about the latter's behaviour with Sugar: 'I saw you, the both of you, in that bus, all lovey-dovey and whispering and giggling and borrowing each other's lipstick! I saw you!'. Here Gerry seems to be both jealous man and jealous lesbian rival competing for Sugar's favour. Later, on the beach, when Sugar begs 'Shell Oil, Jr' to come to the show at the hotel that night, 'Daphne' says maliciously, if not, indeed, bitchily, 'Yes, do come . . . and bring your yacht!'.

The clearest indication of Gerry's ambiguity with regard to sex and gender occurs, of course, in the episodes with Osgood, especially in his reaction to being pinched by the elderly playboy, and later in his acceptance of Osgood's proposal of marriage. When he tells Joe that he is engaged, Joe asks, 'Who's the lucky girl?', to which Gerry responds ecstatically, 'I am'. Moreover, when Joe instructs Gerry that he cannot marry Osgood, Gerry says plaintively, 'I tell you, I will never find another man who's so good to me'. The line echoes Sugar's tales of the worthlessness of tenor sax players, which take on added irony from the fact that Joe, as 'Shell Oil, Jr', also dumps Sugar, even though he is to all intents and purposes the millionaire she wants to marry and not merely another treacherous tenor sax player. The final irony of the film occurs in Gerry's admission to Osgood that he is not a woman, to which Osgood's nonchalant response that it does not matter ('nobody's perfect') prevents the narrative from closing on the heterosexual norm represented in the background as Joe and Sugar embrace. Instead, it opens up the possibility of a homosexual union between Osgood and Gerry, whose face, in a shot with which the film ends, expresses disbelief and resignation, not anger and outrage.

It is worth considering whether such a story could have been told in film earlier in the decade. Certainly, by locating the time of the action in 1929, the movie places the narrative in a time thirty years distant, and toward the end of a post-World War I era notorious for its free lifestyle, decadence and hedonism. But only four years earlier than *Some Like It Hot*, in *Rebel Without a Cause* (1955), Jim Stark (James Dean)—self-destructive and searching desperately for values he can believe in—expresses grief and contempt for his father whose emasculation is symbolically represented in his wearing a frilly apron in one scene, and in his capitulation, until almost the end of the film, to his shrewish wife's demands and complaints. At one point, Jim begs him to be a man, and to stand up to his wife. Here we may read the presence of an uncertainty about masculine norms and values precipitated, as we saw in Chapter 1, by the consequences of World War II. The threat of homosexuality in *Rebel Without a Cause*, represented by the adulation of Jim by Plato (Sal Mineo), is neutralised in three ways. First, Plato is constructed as a neurotic and hence not a model to be imitated or encouraged. Second, in one scene he is infantilised, playing son to Jim and Judy (Natalie Wood), and thus rendered harmless, if annoying. Third, and most convincingly, he is shot dead by the police at the end of the film. The sharp difference between this film's treatment of the (potentially) homosexual and *Some Like It Hot* reinforces the idea that *Rebel Without a Cause* articulates the greater anxiety felt by men in the years immediately following the war. By 1959, however, that anxiety seems to be less of an issue. *Some Like It Hot* is able to treat the matters of cross-dressing and implied homosexuality comically without constructing these as a serious threat to the dominant model of masculinity. Indeed, we might say that the comic treatment allows the otherwise threatening and taboo topic of homosexuality to be foregrounded more positively than in the earlier film.

Though today we tend to think of a comedy as a narrative or a performance with a lot of laughs scattered through it, in traditional, classical terms the genre of comedy is a narrative which begins with dissonance and trouble and ends with happiness and the resolution of all difficulties. Typically, comic closure is effected by means of a romantic union, with either marriage or the promise of marriage. In *Some Like It Hot*, one element of the narrative line does indeed close that way: this is the union between Joe and Sugar, passionately kissing in the rear of the launch. However, the foregrounded element—though it, too, promises union and marriage—is a source of consternation to Gerry, and remains a troublesome idea, given the dominant model of masculinity as purely heterosexual. The failure of *Some Like It Hot* to close definitively on heterosexuality is thus reinforced by its double comic narrative structure, resolving the difficulties of romance for Sugar and Joe, but complicating them humorously for Gerry and Osgood. The facts that *Some Like It Hot* is funny and that heterosexuality is vindicated in the union of Joe and Sugar do not completely defuse the highly subversive nature of the film's ending.

4

W(h)ither Masculinity?

Cultural texts are more than simple narratives or images. They reflect models and ideologies abroad in the culture, and (by giving these form through narrative, example and illustration) reinforce them and refract them back to the culture. A circuit is thus established whereby unjust, unpleasant or simply illogical patterns of behaviour may become canonised for members of the culture. This is not quite analogous to the idea, frequently aired, that violence on television produces violence on the street and in the home. Such a view in its popular form assumes too simple a correlation between what young people see on the television or cinema screen and how they behave. It posits, in other words, a directly causal relationship articulated through simple imitation. More likely, violence on television (or in the cinema) confirms what young people already 'know' about violence and its relation to masculinity, namely that it is manly to be strong, that the strong conquer, that victory is better than defeat, and so on. In this way, violence in the popular media feeds back into the more general, and hence more diffuse, model of masculinity, thus reinforcing and legitimising it. There are dangers in this: first, that repeated representations of such behaviour will naturalise it, and second, that any criticism of it will be deflected and therefore never questioned.

As we have seen in our exploration of *Duke Bluebeard's Castle*, *Tootsie* and *Some Like It Hot*, gender matters are not exempt from such representation and naturalisation. Moreover, even where a text consciously sets out (as in *Tootsie*) to interrogate the naturalisation of a set of assumptions, there may still remain a residue of gender ideology which is itself not interrogated. Feminist critics are thus perfectly correct in pointing out that—at least until comparatively recently—issues to do with masculinity customarily have been taken for granted, not only in the range of texts available but also in discussions about them. Consequently, men are neither invited nor encouraged to examine their own assumptions and actions, except under extraordinary circumstances, as, for instance, when a relationship of some kind goes awry or a spate of violence captures the public's attention.

The codes by which masculinity may be represented are both formal and informal. For instance, formal codes are often to be found and given substance in the law. An example of this is the set of regulations pertaining to pornography or obscenity, which usually prohibits the representation of the penis in materials available to a wide sector of the public. In some countries or states any such representation would be legally actionable; in other places, however, it is the representation of the *erect* penis which is prohibited. It is thus assumed that the young and the sensitive will be shocked or in some other way traumatised by the sight of the penis, flaccid or erect, though, interestingly, the sight of the nude female body and genitals apparently does not have the same effect.

Informal codes by which masculinity may be represented are, by contrast, often only implicit. We can think of them as defining, by traditional example and precept, a kind of folk-wisdom about how men and masculinity may be conceived. For instance, though men experience excruciating agony when transfixed by a sharp, penetrating weapon (whether a sword, a spear, a bayonet or, for that matter, a bullet), it is not usual to represent them positively as screaming or doubled over in pain, though this would be the normal response to such an event. Instead, men are generally shown to be stoic, bearing their agony discreetly, dismissing mortal wounds as mere scratches, and thinking of others—family, girlfriend, home, another soldier—rather than themselves. This is part of the construction of the masculine as heroic. Those men, however, who *are* shown as having normal responses to pain are often constructed as cowards, namby-pambies, or 'the enemy', often by definition less stoic and heroic than 'our side'; more positively, they may be merely adjunct characters, like the hero's offsider in a western.

This is not to say that no men have ever demonstrated this ideal stoicism and heroism. The real question is this: would they have behaved thus if the demands of the model did not require it of them, if there were not a myriad representations in the culture of how a man should behave in adversity and, where death becomes inevitable, how he should die nobly? The textual representation of gender behaviour is therefore an extremely powerful factor in the way that real people behave. There is thus a reciprocal relationship between actual behaviour and the representation of behaviour: the latter may reflect (or be thought to reflect) the former, but it may also influence the former. This is a truth that those involved in commercial advertising and in political propaganda have long understood and exploited.

The outcome of a recent lawsuit offers an interesting case illustrating the issues of gender ideology, behaviour, representation and the power of such representation. The *Australian* newspaper ran two stories on this event in its issue of 11 February 1993. The first, 'ET Awarded $350,000 Damages' (AAP, 1993:2), is matter-of-fact, and is attributed to AAP (Australian Associated Press). The second, which appears in the 'Features' section of the paper and is titled 'The Crotch of the Matter' (Harari, 1993:11), not only gives more detail, but in its tone and side-remarks contrives to transform the story into an instance of rather juicy gossip laced with ironic, even humorous, commentary. The facts of the matter are as follows. An Australian star Rugby League player, Andrew Ettingshausen (known popularly as 'ET'), sued Australian Consolidated Press (ACP) for publishing in the April 1991 issue of *HQ* magazine a photograph taken during the Kangaroo Rugby League team's tour of Britain and France in 1990, which showed a nude Ettingshausen showering with two other rugby players. He claimed defamation in that the photograph exposed his penis to view, and he was awarded damages of $350 000 by the New South Wales Supreme Court. Those damages are among the highest awarded in Australia for such a legal action (AAP, ibid.).

The basis of Ettingshausen's claim was that he had neither given permission for the publication of the photograph, nor would have done so; and that the photograph, as reproduced in *HQ* (a magazine with a male and female readership in their late twenties), 'showed his penis and held him up to public ridicule and contempt'. The jury, made up of two men and two women, also found that 'the publication carried another defamatory imputation to people who knew that at that time Ettingshausen was the NSW Rugby League's schools and junior development promotions officer' (ibid.).

The stance and tone adopted by the author of the second article, Fiona Harari, suggest strongly that, from a woman's perspective, the Ettingshausen affair was both a bit of a storm in a teacup and a lesson to men about the objectification of the body which women have traditionally been expected to endure as natural and inevitable. The interesting issues in the Ettingshausen story for a student of masculinity centre on the question of why a photograph of a nude man which exposes his penis to the viewer should be defamatory of its subject. No doubt there is a range of legal niceties which the counsels for Mr Ettingshausen and the ACP rehearsed before the court; and one can, of course, sympathise with Ettingshausen's claim (reported in Harari's piece) that it was humiliating to be asked by young women to sign the photograph in the magazine. Not to be dismissed either is Ettingshausen's plea that his function as schools and junior development promotions officer was jeopardised by such a publication. Nevertheless, there remains the matter of why a photograph of a nude man might be construed as defamatory by the culture—such an understanding then being articulated authoritatively through the court's decision.

There are two ways in which this question may be answered. The first has to do with publicly representing (or, more properly, with the prohibition against publicly representing) the penis. In a patriarchal culture, the anatomical fact of sexual difference is translated into a social fact, which may be expressed thus: those with a penis may have access to power, those without may not. A stipulation of this kind thus automatically excludes women, but, as we have seen, does not automatically include all men. Rather, men must compete with one another for access to power, which is in any case distributed differentially rather than evenly among the competitors. Some men—gays, for example—may be debarred on ideological grounds. That is, a man who, aside from his sexual proclivities, is in every respect like his heterosexual fellows in manner, aggressiveness, drive, competitiveness, athleticism and so on, may still be regarded with suspicion and contempt, marginalised and even prosecuted on the grounds of his sexuality. What is at issue here is not that man's qualifications as a social being but his sexual identity, which, though private, is transformed into a social disability by a masculine ideology which requires every man to be heterosexual.

In such a structure, the penis becomes more than a marker of sexual difference: it becomes a social symbol. As such, it is represented as erect, swollen as much with power as blood. This representation of the penis is generally called, in gender theory, the *phallus*, and we should note that it is to be distinguished from the actual penis. 'Phallus' derives from the Latin and Greek terms for the penis. In gender theory, however, the distinction between *anatomical fact* and *social symbol* is generally preserved by referring to the former as 'penis' and to the latter as 'phallus', which is always imagined as larger and more powerful than any actual penis could be. Indeed, the phallus is not only the symbolisation of male power, it also becomes the goal of male endeavour. To attain and wield the power of the phallus is the motivation underlying much male behaviour, which in turn produces *phallocentrism*, a key term in feminist theory. The word does not mean literally that men think about nothing but their penises (though no doubt some do), but rather that the penis is symbolic of the phallus and its power. It is thus the means by which men may gain access to that power, a means which is not available to women as it is to men.

The phallus may be invoked in different ways. We have all heard of phallic symbols: guns, sports cars, Harley Davidson motorbikes, cigars, and so on; Duke Bluebeard's keys might be interpreted as such symbols. However, positions and acts of power may also be understood as other kinds, perhaps less obvious, of phallic symbols. Indeed, some of these are often associated with items more generally understood as phallic. Think, for instance, of the policeman's truncheon (interestingly, and probably not accidentally, also known as his 'nightstick'), which becomes the detailed expression of the masculine and phallic power of a corps of men licensed by the state to control the citizenry. We might also recall in this connection that the glans-like shape of the traditional English bobby's helmet transforms the entire man into a phallic object. Importantly, then, phallic power may also be displaced on to and symbolised by the male body. Strong, muscular physiques become expressions of such power, which is one reason why men strain away in gyms to acquire them: they are signs not merely of health and fitness but also of authority over other, less impressively built males.

The man gifted by nature with large genitals thus often acquires the status of a cultural totem because he is seen as inherently a strong claimant to the power of the phallus. Significantly, it seems to be mostly men who are concerned with penis size. Women, by contrast, are frequently cited in professional journal articles, in sex manuals and in popular women's magazines as finding the giant penis aesthetically repugnant, physically uncomfortable or painful during intercourse, and/or merely ridiculous. That it is principally a male preoccupation, moreover, is confirmed by the fascination expressed by many gay men with penis size: we should remember that homosexual men are subjected to the same cultural and social conditioning as male heterosexuals, and thus often articulate similar anxieties and focuses of concern.

It would thus be possible to argue that gay men are, ironically, *more* masculine than straight men in that the homosexual fascination with the penis (and with the large penis) is in some way 'purer' than its heterosexual equivalent, since it is part of an all-male discourse, uncontaminated, as it were, by reference to the female. In addition, the intriguing—and dangerous—question also arises of whether the general anxiety of men about penis size (and the figuring of the penis through a wide range of various phallic symbols and objects) indicates a latent homo-eroticism built into masculinity, a homo-eroticism repressed and disavowed because, of course, it conflicts with the issue of patriarchal power.

Given all this male attention to and concern with phallic power, it is not surprising that the male genitals become taboo. Since no man's actual penis can ever compete with the splendour, majesty and power of the imaginary phallus, the penis is thus better suggested than actually depicted or revealed. Its revelation can only expose its owner to invidious comparisons. And so the penis—particularly when erect, a condition which reveals its size more accurately than when it remains flaccid—becomes forbidden, defined as obscene and pornographic.

And so we return to the Ettingshausen affair. Despite the facts that he possesses a magnificent physique (in the magazine story he was described as a Greek god, according to Harari), and that he is a prominent and proficient player in one of the rougher male contact sports (details that qualify him as a favourite contender in the Masculinity Stakes), Ettingshausen's case rested on the claim that the exposure of his penis 'defamed' him. This we may understand to mean that, with his genitals on display, the player's access to phallic power was threatened by comparison with the symbolic phallus, thus exposing him to ridicule. This tallies with and explains the subsequent joshing of Ettingshausen by his fellow players: 'Later, when posing for team photos, players taunted him with comments such as "Hang your cock out, ET" and "Make sure you don't get ET's cock in the photograph"'(Harari, ibid.).

Unwanted comparisons of this kind, incidentally, may not be restricted to our culture. In classical Greek art, for example, nude male statues often had small genitals when they represented youths or gods, but displayed large and grotesque penises when representing satyrs and the like. The usual explanation is that the Greeks regarded the intellect as superior to the passions of the body, so that it was only the bestial being, like the satyr, who was shown with enormous genitals, to signify that his baser instincts ruled his mind and will. Certainly, there is plenty of evidence of such an ideology in what writing has survived from those times. However, we may conjecture that this doctrine is likewise a strategy to account for the discrepancy between the actual penis and the imaginary phallus.

An irony emerging from Harari's reporting of the trial centres on the debate as to whether or not the plaintiff's penis was clearly in view in the photograph. No matter how embarrassing it might be to confront a public which had seen the photograph, how much more demeaning must it have been to suffer a prolonged debate in court about whether a mere shadowing in the photograph might or might not have been one's penis, and whether the shadow was so placed anatomically as to constitute the probability that it *was* one's penis! If the individual penis can indeed never equal the imaginary phallus, for a man to hear learned counsel and testifying witnesses contesting the actual existence of his penis must be extremely belittling, of both his ego and his sense of phallic worth.

The second way of answering the question of why the publication of a nude photograph might defame its subject involves the male body as the object of the gaze. We may distinguish, in discourses of all kinds, between the discursive *subject* and *object*. The subject of a discourse is the one who thinks, speaks or acts the terms of the discourse, while the object is that which is thought, spoken or acted on. The subject is thus enabled by the power structure relevant to the discourse, while the object remains relatively or absolutely powerless. In the gender discourse of a culture dominated by men and male concerns, the subject of much discourse tends to be male: thus, until quite recently, the subjects of discourses like the law, medicine, government and commerce, for instance, were generally thought of as male. In this way, the discourses implied that these occupations were male preserves. It is still possible today to hear murmurs of discontent and disapproval when a woman is appointed to a high government office, or is promoted into a position of responsibility (which implies power): that woman is regarded as usurping the domain (represented in the discourse) of the masculine.

One prominent aspect of the discourse of gender is that which defines the subject and object of the discourse of sexual desire, an issue with which feminist theory and politics has been grappling for several decades now. Perhaps its clearest representation, not surprisingly, is to be found in pornography, which generally assumes a male viewing position and hence a male subjectivity. This, given the logic of the discourse and its associated lines of power, inevitably privileges the masculine, so that the woman depicted (in heterosexual pornography) becomes the discursive object, something to be gazed at and aroused by, but not to be accorded any subjectivity of her own. For to do the latter would be to acknowledge that she has her own power and mobility, and a voice in the discourse. Similarly, the daily harassment of a sexual nature which a woman might endure walking past a construction site, say, or dealing with male superiors in the office or confronting a patronising door-to-door salesman might not be overtly erotic, but it positions her none the less as a discursive object relative to men's discursive subjectivity.

What of the male body which becomes the focus of the viewer's gaze? There is clearly a danger here for men, which is why those males whose livelihood depends on the objectification (and commercialisation) of their bodies—say, actors and models—are often thought of as feminised (or 'prostituted', which is pretty much the same thing in our culture's scale of values). The male body in gay pornography is similarly objectified, rendered like the female body to the male viewer. Of course, there are strategies to minimise or deflect the consequences of exhibiting the male body. Nude statues, for instance, can be so composed as to overpower the viewer through sheer size, as we see in Michelangelo's *David*;[1] or the features of the statue can be represented as suggesting thought turned inward, as is the case with Rodin's *The Thinker*. The male body can be represented as engaged in an activity which confers upon it a recognisable male subjectivity, however fictitious or spurious. The same is true of gay pornographic images: whereas the body which is simply displayed for viewing or splayed for sexual intercourse is often constructed as feminised because objectified, the body which is self-absorbed (as in images representing masturbation) or intent upon penetrating another body is often thought of as masculine, because retaining some semblance of subjectivity.

Ettingshausen is familiar Australia-wide not only through his performance on the rugby field but also through his appearances in the media as a model in advertisements for a variety of products, including men's clothing. He thus runs the risk of becoming that anathematised thing, the male object of the gaze. Many of his appearances in television commercials and other sorts of advertisement evade the simple objectification of his body, and hence of his discursive position, by some of the strategies considered above. However, a *nude* photograph of the famous Ettingshausen body invites his transformation into an eroticised object of the gaze. In this way, therefore, the player may well have felt, however obscurely, that he had been humiliated and hence defamed.

And we might read his taking the matter to court as an attempt to regain his subjectivity in the midst of the various discourses—of gender, sexuality, the law, the rights of the individual, visual representation and so on—that his action invoked. But the discussion about whether or not the Ettingshausen penis was visible in the offending photograph inevitably neutralised that attempt, and drew the hapless player back into the domain of the object. Certainly, popular comment in the media and on the street indicated that Ettingshausen's credibility may have been irreparably damaged, since such comment tended generally to run along the lines of 'He shows his body half-naked anyway, so why is he now worrying about a little nudity?'. By allowing his body to be viewed as an object, Ettingshausen was deemed, apparently, to have forfeited his claim to subjectivity, and hence to control over that body. It became, as it were, public property.

The Ettingshausen case throws suggestively into relief a number of the concerns and anxieties that beset men trying to live according to the dominant model of masculinity, not the least of which is the positioning of the male as the object of a gaze which on the one hand supervises and disciplines and on the other may also articulate desire.[2] Moreover, the story also hints that, for all masculinity's pervasive tyranny over both men and women in the culture, its superiority and power rest on fragile, even treacherous, foundations. It does not in fact take much to produce a defensive reaction from men—the presence of a determined woman with a political agenda, an openly gay man, or the imputation of femininity often suffice. This suggests, in turn, that the very tyranny of the patriarchal model of masculinity masks an uncertainty felt by many men but which the model itself dictates should not be expressed.[3]

For the demands made of men by the model and the discourse of patriarchal masculinity are as damaging as those made of women, but in different ways. The cultural models of masculinity and of femininity, together with the appropriate social behaviours, are each constructed by patriarchy and hence are men-oriented. Femininity, for women, has traditionally been a set of behaviours to please men and reinforce the dominant–subordinate relationship of men to women in society. In many ways, therefore, how women should look and behave has been explicitly prescribed by male cultural ideology and erotic preferences, defining, for instance, whether women should be young, blonde or brunette, pretty, acquiescent, soft and yielding, whether they should have large breasts or ample hips, and so on. Other factors determining female· behaviour have included the social consequences of non-compliance. These include the emotional and/or sexual rejection of women (here we may group the 'old maid' syndrome, for which there is no real male equivalent); the punishment of women as disobedient (and hence as demonstrating that they have minds and wills of their own); the labelling of women as either 'castrating bitches' (that is, not only do they have minds and wills of their own, they have the determination to get their own way) or 'bull (or diesel) dykes' (that is, if a woman does not succumb to a man's advances, it must be because of her own sexual or physical 'abnormality').

When women rebel against these conditions and limitations, therefore, they question both the patriarchal structure which imposes them and the men who mediate that structure in real social terms. There is, in other words, an 'Other' who makes such demands of women, and that 'Other' may be defined negatively and absolutely as an enemy or, more simply, as an antagonist who operates, knowingly or unknowingly, as the tool of a much larger and more powerful structure.[4] For men within patriarchy, however, the 'Other' is not only women but also other men. To wish to be acknowledged as 'masculine' places men neatly in a dilemma, for it requires them to accept both the terms of patriarchal masculinity and the supervision by men in general, together with their (often informal and unstated) judgement of the individual. Failure to comply with the former necessarily invokes the latter.

Efforts (or instructions) aimed at producing co-operation among men often attempt to neutralise or at least mask the highly competitive nature of masculinity. But the latter generally remains intractable. Thus, though we may expect one team to win over another in a football match, we also judge who was best player in that team, and, indeed, who was 'Man of the Match'. Similarly, although employees of a business may be given a pep talk on how the organisation is really a team or a family, there are often prizes for the 'Best Employee of the Month (or Year)'. Thus the potentially co-operative behaviour of men is undermined by competitiveness, and the effort to encourage co-operation contradicted by the recognition-and-reward dynamic built into the discourse. We might note here that such rewards may be attributed also to the competitiveness encouraged by capitalism in an industrial and business-oriented society. This suggests very strongly that the development of the modern patriarchal model of masculinity is closely tied to the development of modern capitalism—not that patriarchal masculinity did not hold sway before the rise of capitalism, but rather that it found a congruence with the new order, adapted itself and evolved accordingly.

For the traditional and dominant model to continue to function successfully, the social and cultural climate must remain favourable; but that climate has been changing, in many ways, for some time. While women (of whatever sexual inclination) and gays have been developing a politics and a vision that necessarily require a shift in values and a loosening of former attitudes, many men continue to cling to a model that is fast becoming difficult to sustain. This is understandable. We often tend to hang on to what we know for fear that the unknown will overwhelm us. That men find it difficult to dislodge the idol of traditional masculinity and topple it from its high place is therefore to be expected. That many—women, gay men, and those straight men who desire a new model of masculinity— become impatient with the delay in dismantling the older model is also understandable, for it means that many people are held in an interim state, half free from but still half shackled to the old beliefs and practices.

It may be a little premature for any confidence that real change is taking place. Events in the structure and dynamics of a culture's gender system depend, as we have seen, on many other things happening at the same time. Many of the triumphs of the women's, lesbian and gay movements, some of whose conditions of emergence we considered in Chapter 1, were made possible by additional factors, such as a general political unrest and dissatisfaction with governments around the world; by a booming economy; and by growth in the area of education, in terms both of the numbers being educated and the introduction into the curriculum of new material often hitherto considered 'non-educational', such as feminism. In a world whose economy seems to become more depressed each day, however, such factors come to be considered not only luxuries but even politically subversive. The swing in recent decades to conservative governments in the western world suggests that a dogma is in force which assumes that former and therefore familiar conditions can be re-created today, and that these will of necessity bring about a positive change in social, cultural and economic dynamics.

Curiously—and ironically—much of the change which men may find difficult to accept as inevitable or just or natural is often the consequence of earlier choices and activities made by men themselves. Take the instance of the changes in domestic arrangements after World War II: these were a response to a situation—war— initiated by men. The point here is not that that war ought not to have been fought, or that it was the fault purely and simply of 'men', which suggests that all men were implicated and that therefore all men, living and dead, are to blame. Rather, the very fact of the war itself changed the meaning and the values of the style of existence which the men went to battle to protect and to perpetuate.

Some change is being wrought also by men's self-examination. Men's groups, courses in men's studies and books about men, like this one, as well as courses and books about homosexuality enable men to venture out of the carapace of acceptable attitudes and practices imposed by the dominant model of masculinity, and to compare their experiences and feelings with those of other men as well as women. These opportunities provide a variety of structures by which the notion of masculinity can be abstracted from everyday behaviour and expectations, and examined, tested and criticised as grounded in a culture's history and ideology. Presumably, if enough men take advantage of these forums of research and debate, further change can be effected in those social structures which pertain to gender, and in ways of thinking culturally about them.

Recent developments in gender theory suggest further possibilities. Judith Butler, for instance, queries the apparently natural inevitability of associating 'man' and 'masculine' with the male body, or 'woman' and 'feminine' with the female one (Butler, 1990:6). This disengaging of actual bodies from culturally imagined and imposed gender requirements points to the possibility of abolishing the link conventionally maintained between masculinity and male heterosexuality, so that male homosexuality will no longer be defined as producing that apparent paradox, a non-masculine yet male subject.

The question often arises of whether the current focus on men's studies is merely a protective reflex response to feminism or a moment of chic male self-reflection. Both of these options assume the transience of the interest. In the case of the reflex response, the expectation is that feminism will die away as a vogue in the natural course of things, taking the troubling interest in masculinity with it; and, in the case of the self-reflective response, the expectation is a return sooner or later from an embarrassingly confessional and self-examining fashion among men to business as usual. Obviously, much depends on historical conjuncture and what circumstances prevail. Perhaps, if political trends move further still toward the right, older values will continue to be paraded and reinforced, if not, indeed, enforced. In that case, it may well be that both feminism and the newly emergent study and theorisation of masculinity will be silenced, although one hopes that this will be neither a final event nor a quiet, ignorable one. A more troubling possibility is that such study will be co-opted in order to reinstate the old concept of masculinity with a more explicit and plausible rationale. But now that the process of men's self-examination, self-study and self-criticism has started, it seems likely that reactionary responses to women's rights and to the interrogation of traditional masculine discourse may be a rearguard action only.

What might a new masculinity look like? When confronted with this question, theorists of masculinity are generally a little more cautious than the proponents of either a Bly-esque notion of masculinity or a fairly simple New Age model. We can imagine, however, a number of possibilities that would contribute to such a new masculinity. For instance, we might expect that in the future men will have learned that difference does not also mean superiority or inferiority. To have been born with a penis is an accident of nature, specifically of genetics, and therefore should not be invested with special privilege and power. We might recall, in this regard, that the foetus remains female until fairly late in its development, when hormonal activity triggered by a particular chromosomal combination can change its sex. That men generally are taller and have larger and more powerful physiques than women is the result of evolutionary development, not a mysterious sanctioning of male claims to power. Indeed, extremely tall and/or big men are regarded rather as oddities, and not necessarily as more masculine because of their height or size; this confirms that the criteria are relative and not absolute ones.

Moreover, that some men are attracted to other men and not to women is a fact that is neither as freakish nor as rare as current homophobic attitudes would have it; nor are male homosexuals any the less 'men' on account of their sexual inclinations. The brouhaha created in 1992 by the Australian Labor Government's decision to lift the ban on gays in the armed forces—and in 1993 by President Bill Clinton's effort to fulfil his election campaign promise to do the same in his country—indicates an extraordinary ignorance of the fact that gays have always been present in the military organisation of any state or nation. Absence of information about whether there are gays in the armed forces, and if so how many, does not mean that the gays themselves are absent. Moreover, some homosexuals have even been elevated to the status of hero, as the case of T. E. Lawrence ('Lawrence of Arabia') attests, thus putting paid to the vulgar notion that such men are sissies and poor soldier material. Further, the storm of protest (particularly from the military establishment) over gays in the armed forces betrays an equally astonishing lack of knowledge of military history. One of the most respected and feared military units in ancient Greece was the Sacred Band of Thebes, made up of 300 pairs of male lovers, which defeated Sparta at the battles of Leuctra in 371 BC and Mantinea in 362 BC, and which fought to the last man against Philip of Macedon at Chaeronea in 338 BC. A new masculinity might greet the information that a man has a sexual preference for other men in the same spirit as the news that so-and-so prefers one food, or one colour, to another.

We might hope, too, that men in the future will more truly co-operate with and care for one another, and reject the cycles of rivalry (often expressed through violence or the threat of violence) which mark the current patriarchal model of masculinity. Bartók's Duke, immured in his fears, his sadness, his regrets and his memories only of love and affection, serves as a salutary example of the consequences of that model.

The erasure of the notion of difference between the sexes may be a foolish ambition. Perhaps between men and women there are finally ineradicable and irreducible differences created by anatomical and biological differences; and these too, perhaps, produce very different needs in men and women. But those differences do not have to be translated into a scale of social values which in turn creates untenable and frequently intolerable conditions of existence for women and men in society and which produces a politics of advantage and disadvantage founded less on moral merit than on biological accident. The phallus, if it must survive, need not be a source of anxiety and fear as well as fascination to all. Instead, it might remain a simple sign of the biological difference between men and women, but by no means the only one of importance.

Notes

1 Masculinities and identities

[1] This irony was pointed out to me by Mr Steve Singer.

[2] I am indebted for this information to Dr T. Gidley, of Hollywood Hospital, the Repatriation General Hospital in Perth, Western Australia. Any errors of detail are mine, not his.

[3] According to documentation provided for a workshop on the International Year of the Family (1994), only approximately 28 per cent of Australian households conform to the nuclear-family model. Most families are of the single-parent, blended, fostered or some other non-nuclear type (Department of Health, Housing and Community Services, 1992:4).

[4] Obviously such categories are not hermetic. Thus the John Bly response, for instance, may be seen as both petitional and penitential in part.

[5] This phrase interestingly suggests that gender identity is donned like clothing. In other words, it is possible for a homosexual man to 'pass' as a heterosexual by adopting the appropriate gender behaviour in order to cloak his non-normative sexual orientation.

2 'Light must end the reign of darkness'

[1] I am indebted to Robert Curry, of the Conservatorium of the Western Australian Academy of the Performing Arts, for providing the background information about the opera.

2   The translation used is that by Chester Kallman in the libretto accompanying the Decca recording indicated in the list of references and suggested further reading at the end of this book.

3   Paul Griffiths suggests that the narrative sources and influences behind Bartók's opera are not so much the account of the historical Bluebeard, Gilles de Retz (who figures, for instance, in J.-K. Huysmans' novel *Là-bas*, written in 1891), as, first, the version related in Perrault's collection of fairy tales *Histoires ou contes du temps passé* (1697; the translation by Robert Samber in *Histories, or Tales of past Times* [1729] is included in Opie, 1980:137–41); and, second, the libretto written by the Symbolist poet Maeterlinck for Dukas' opera *Ariane et Barbe-Bleue* (*Ariadne and Bluebeard*, 1907), in which, incidentally, seven doors also feature (Griffiths, 1984:58–9). The latter text may well have suggested the symbolic nature of the castle in Bartók's opera.

4   It is always worth testing the merit of 'naturally' when it comes up in speech or writing. In many instances, the word signifies an ideologically created sense of inevitability, rather than one actually caused by or created in nature. See John Boswell's discussion of 'natural' versus 'unnatural' with reference to the debate about homosexuality (Boswell, 1980:11–15).

3 'Well, nobody's perfect'

1   The dialogue quoted is transcribed from a commercial video recording of the film.

4 W(h)ither masculinity?

1   Some readers might object that, given Michelangelo's own homosexuality, the *David* provides a poor example. But we should remember that the statue was a commissioned work for public display, and that therefore it employs the codes appropriate to its purpose.

2   The notion of the supervising and disciplining gaze is developed by Michel Foucault in *Discipline and Punish: The Birth of the Prison* (1977). Other theorists of the gaze include Laura Mulvey, whose 'Visual Pleasure and Narrative Cinema', originally pub-

lished in *Screen*, 16, 3, 1975, pp. 6–18, is usefully included in a *Screen* reader (*Screen*, 1992:22–34), together with other essays, for example, by John Ellis, who also has theorised the gaze.

3   Interestingly, the Ettingshausen case was reopened in October of the same year after an appeal by the magazine's publisher against the jury's verdict. The New South Wales Court of Appeal found the amount of damages to be excessive.

4   The 'Other' in feminist theory generally refers to woman, distinguished discursively from the 'Self' or 'Same' that is man and the subject of cultural discourse. The 'Self' is constructed as unified and unitary, the 'Other' multiple and scattered; and that construction not only allows the 'Self' to be the discursive subject, it also enables the 'Self' to become occulted and invisible as a construct, so that it comes to be identified as the natural position. See, for instance, Luce Irigaray, 'This Sex Which Is Not One' (Marks and De Courtivron, 1980:99–106).

Bibliography

The following bibliography is not exhaustive; rather, it is representative of the range of material on gender, and on masculinity in particular. The most recent research in the field, however, is usually to be found in the periodical literature. One periodical focusing specifically on masculinity, *The Journal of Men's Studies: A Scholarly Journal About Men and Masculinities*, commenced publication in 1992 (enquiries, submissions of articles for publication and subscriptions should be addressed to Dr James A. Doyle, P.O. Box 32, Harriman, TN 37748, USA). Other journals deal more broadly with gender issues, for instance *Genders* or *Journal of Gender Studies*, while still others are concerned with questions of sexuality, for example *Journal of the History of Sexuality*. Some feminist journals from time to time publish special-topic issues which deal with matters pertinent to the study of masculinity, for instance the issue 'Queer Theory: Lesbian and Gay Sexualities', *differences*, 3, 2, 1991 or 'The Phallus Issue', *differences*, 4, 1, 1992. Other journals sometimes publish special-topic issues on masculinity, as is the case with *Southern Review*, 25, 2, 1992. *GLQ (Gay and Lesbian Quarterly)* is a new journal whose inaugural issue is forthcoming. And many journals with broader or different focuses often include articles relevant to the study of gender and/or masculinity. In addition, a number of local publications on men's issues have appeared in various places around the world, with differing degrees of circulation and longevity. In Australia, *XY: Men, Sex, Politics* is distributed nationally (enquiries, subscriptions and submission of manuscripts should be addressed to PO Box 26, Ainslie, ACT 2602, Australia).

Printed sources

Abbott, Franklin (ed.) (1990) *Men and Intimacy: Personal Accounts Exploring the Dilemmas of Modern Male Sexuality*, Freedom, CA: The Crossing Press
— (ed.) (1987) *New Men, New Minds: Breaking Male Tradition. How Today's Men Are Changing the Traditional Rule of Masculinity*, Freedom, CA: The Crossing Press
Abelove, Henry et al. (eds) (1993) *The Lesbian and Gay Studies Reader*, New York and London: Routledge
Ackroyd, Peter (1979) *Dressing Up. Transvestism and Drag: The History of an Obsession*, London: Thames & Hudson
Adam, Barry D. (1987) *The Rise of a Gay and Lesbian Movement*, Boston: Twayne
Altman, Dennis (1986) *AIDS and the New Puritanism*, London: Pluto
— (1973; orig. pub. 1971) *Homosexual: Oppression and Liberation*, London: Penguin
Ariès, Philippe and André Béjin (eds) (1985) *Western Sexuality: Practice and Precept in Past and Present Times*, Oxford: Blackwell
A[ustralian] A[ssociated] P[ress] (1993) 'ET Awarded $350,000 Damages', *Australian*, 11 February, p. 2
Bakhtin, Mikhail (1984; orig. Russian pub. 1964) *Rabelais and His World*, trans. Hélène Iswolsky, Bloomington: Indiana University Press
Barinaga, Marcia (1991) 'Is Homosexuality Biological?', *Science*, 253, August, pp. 956–7
Bly, Robert (1991) *Iron John: A Book About Men*, Shaftesbury, Dorset, and Rockport, Mass.: Element Books
Boone, Joseph A. and Michael Cadden (eds) (1990) *Engendering Men: The Question of Male Feminist Criticism*, New York and London: Routledge
Bornoff, Nicholas (1991) *Pink Samurai: The Pursuit and Politics of Sex in Japan*, London: Grafton-HarperCollins
Boswell, John (1980) *Christianity, Social Tolerance, and Homo-*

sexuality: Gay People in Western Europe from the Beginning of the Christian Era to the Fourteenth Century, Chicago and London: University of Chicago Press

Bray, Alan (1982) *Homosexuality in Renaissance England*, London: Gay Men's Press

Brittan, Arthur (1989) *Masculinity and Power*, Oxford: Blackwell

Brod, Harry (ed.) (1987) *The Making of Masculinities: The New Men's Studies*, London: Allen & Unwin

— (1991; orig. pub. 1984) 'Eros Thanatized: Pornography and Male Sexuality', in Michael S. Kimmel (ed.) *Men Confront Pornography*, New York: Crown Publishers, pp. 190–206

Buchbinder, David (1991) 'Pornography and Male Homosocial Desire: The Case of the New Men's Studies', *Social Semiotics: A Transdisciplinary Journal in Functional Linguistics, Semiotics and Critical Theory*, 1, 2, pp. 51–68

Buchbinder, Howard et al. (1987) *Who's On Top? The Politics of Heterosexuality*, Toronto: Garamond Press

Butler, Judith (1990) *Gender Trouble: Feminism and the Subversion of Identity*, New York and London: Routledge

Carrigan, Tim et al. (1987; orig. pub. 1985) 'Hard and Heavy: Toward a New Sociology of Masculinity', in Michael Kaufman (ed.) *Beyond Patriarchy: Essays by Men on Pleasure, Power, and Change*, Toronto and New York: Oxford University Press, pp. 139–92

Carter, Angela (1981) 'The Bloody Chamber' in *The Bloody Chamber and Other Stories*, London: Penguin, pp. 7–41

Chapman, Rowena and Jonathan Rutherford (eds) (1988) *Male Order: Unwrapping Masculinity*, London: Lawrence & Wishart

Colling, Terry (1992), *Beyond Mateship: Understanding Australian Men*, Sydney: Simon & Schuster Australia

Comstock, Gary David (1991) *Violence Against Lesbians and Gay Men*, New York: Columbia University Press

Connell, R. W. (1987) *Gender and Power: Society, the Person and Sexual Politics*, Sydney: Allen & Unwin

Connell, R. W. and G. W. Dowsett (eds) (1992), *Rethinking Sex: Social Theory and Sexuality Research*, Melbourne: Melbourne University Press

Craig, Steve (ed.) (1992) *Men, Masculinity, and the Media*, Newbury Park: Sage

Cranny-Francis, Anne (1992) *Engendered Fictions: Analysing Gender in the Production and Reception of Texts*, Sydney: New South Wales University Press

Cruikshank, Margaret (1992) *The Gay and Lesbian Liberation Movement*, New York and London: Routledge

Davidson, Arnold I. (1987) 'Sex and the Emergence of Sexuality', *Critical Inquiry*, 14, pp. 16–48

Day, Gary and Clive Bloom (eds) (1988) *Perspectives on Pornography: Sexuality in Film and Literature*, Basingstoke and London: Macmillan

Demény, János (ed.) (1971) *Béla Bartók Letters*, trans. Péter Balabán and István Farkas, rev. Elisabeth West and Colin Mason, New York: St Martin's Press

Department of Health, Housing and Community Services (1992) *Towards International Year of the Family: An Issues Paper Presented to the Community Organisation Support Program International Year of the Family Workshop*, Canberra: Commonwealth of Australia

Dollimore, Jonathan (1991) *Sexual Dissidence: Augustine to Wilde*, Freud to Foucault, Oxford: Clarendon

Dover, K. J. (1989) *Greek Homosexuality. Updated and with a New Postscript*, Cambridge, Mass.: Harvard University Press

Duberman, Martin Bauml et al. (eds) (1989) *Hidden from History: Reclaiming the Gay and Lesbian Past*, New York: NAL-Penguin

Dworkin, Andrea (1989) *Pornography: Men Possessing Women*, New York: Dutton

Dynes, Wayne R. (ed.) (1990) *Encyclopedia of Homosexuality*, 2 vols, New York and London: Garland Publishing Inc.

Easthope, Antony (1986) *What A Man's Gotta Do: The Masculine Myth in Popular Culture*, London: Paladin-Grafton

Ehrenreich, Barbara (1983) *The Hearts of Men: American Dreams and the Flight from Commitment*, London: Pluto

Epstein, Julia and Kristina Straub (eds) (1991) *Body Guards: The Cultural Politics of Gender Ambiguity*, New York and London: Routledge

Even-Zohar, Itamar (1990) 'The "Literary System"', *Poetics Today*, 11, 1, pp. 27–44

Ewen, David (1955) *Encyclopedia of the Opera*, New York: Hill & Wang, Inc.

Faludi, Susan (1992) *Backlash: The Undeclared War Against Women*, London: Chatto & Windus

Featherstone, Mike et al. (eds) (1991) *The Body: Social Process and Cultural Theory*, London: Sage

Feher, Michael et al. (eds) (1989a) *Fragments for a History of the Body, Part One*, New York: Zone

— (1989b) *Fragments for a History of the Body, Part Two*, New York: Zone

— (1989c) *Fragments for a History of the Body, Part Three*, New York: Zone

Fernbach, David (1981) *The Spiral Path: A Gay Contribution to Human Survival*, Boston: Alyson Publications and London: Gay Men's Press

Formaini, Heather (1990) *Men: The Darker Continent*, London: Heinemann

Foucault, Michel (1977; orig. French pub. 1975) *Discipline and Punish: The Birth of the Prison*, trans. Alan Sheridan, London: Penguin

— (1980; orig. French pub. 1976) *The History of Sexuality*, vol. 1, *An Introduction*, trans. Robert Hurley, New York: Vintage Books-Random House

— (1987; orig. French pub. 1984) *The History of Sexuality*, vol. 2, *The Use of Pleasure*, trans. Robert Hurley, London: Penguin

— (1988; orig. French pub. 1984) *The History of Sexuality*, vol. 3, *The Care of the Self*, trans. Robert Hurley, New York: Vintage-Random

French, Marilyn (1992) *The War Against Women*, London: Penguin

Fussell, Paul (1975) *The Great War and Modern Memory*, London, Oxford and New York: Oxford University Press

— (1989) *Wartime: Understanding and Behavior in the Second World War*, New York and Oxford: Oxford University Press

Garber, Marjorie (1992) *Vested Interests: Cross-Dressing and Cultural Anxiety*, New York and London: Routledge

Gilmore, David D. (1990) *Manhood in the Making: Cultural Concepts of Masculinity*, New Haven and London: Yale University Press

Goodich, Michael (1979) *The Unmentionable Vice: Homosexuality in the Later Medieval Period*, Santa Barbara: Ross-Erikson

Greenberg, David F. (1988) *The Construction of Homosexuality*, Chicago and London: University of Chicago Press

Griffiths, Paul (1984) *The Master Musicians: Bartók*, London and Melbourne: J. M. Dent & Sons Ltd

Hall, Lesley A. (1991) Hidden Anxieties: *Male Sexuality, 1900–1950*, Cambridge: Polity

Halperin, David M. (1990) *One Hundred Years of Homosexuality, and Other Essays on Greek Love*, New York and London: Routledge

Harari, Fiona (1993) 'The Crotch of the Matter', *Australian*, 11 February, p. 11

Hawkes, Ponch (1990) *Best Mates: A Study*, Melbourne: McPhee Gribble

Hearn, Jeff (1987) *The Gender of Oppression: Men, Masculinity and the Critique of Marxism*, Brighton: Wheatsheaf

— and David Morgan (eds) (1990) *Men, Masculinities and Social Theory*, London: Unwin Hyman

Hinsch, Bret (1990) *Passions of the Cut Sleeve: The Male Homosexual Tradition in China*, Berkeley: University of California Press

Hoch, Paul (1979) *White Hero, Black Beast: Racism, Sexism and the Mask of Masculinity*, London: Pluto

Hocquenghem, Guy (1978; orig. French pub. 1972) *Homosexual Desire*, trans. Daniella Dangoor, London: Allison & Busby

Hunter, Ian et al. (1993) *On Pornography: Literature, Sexuality and Obscenity Law*, Basingstoke and London: Macmillan

Hwang, David Henry (1988) *M. Butterfly*, London: Penguin

Kaufman, Michael (ed.) (1987) *Beyond Patriarchy: Essays by Men on Pleasure, Power, and Change*, Toronto and New York: Oxford University Press

Kenna, Peter et al. (1977) *Drag Show: Featuring Peter Kenna's Mates and Steve J. Spears'* The Elocution of Benjamin Franklin, Sydney: Currency

Kimmel, Michael S. (ed.) (1990) *Men Confront Pornography*, New York: Crown Publishers

Kimmel, Michael S. and Michael A. Messner (eds) (1989) *Men's Lives*, New York: Macmillan

Kinsey, Alfred C. et al. (1948) *Sexual Behavior in the Human Male*, Philadelphia: W. B. Saunders

Kroker, Arthur and Marilouise Kroker (eds) (1991) *The Hysterical Male: New Feminist Theory*, Basingstoke and London: Macmillan

Krutnik, Frank (1991) *In a Lonely Street: Film Noir, Genre, Masculinity*, London and New York: Routledge

Laqueur, Thomas (1990) *Making Sex: Body and Gender from the Greeks to Freud*, Cambridge, Mass., and London: Harvard University Press

LeVay, Simon (1991) 'A Difference in Hypothalamic Structure Between Heterosexual and Homosexual Men', *Science,* 253, August, pp. 1034–7

Longhurst, Derek (ed.) (1989) *Reading Popular Fiction: Gender, Genre and Narrative Pleasure*, London: Unwin Hyman

McCann, Graham (1991) *Rebel Males: Clift, Brando and Dean*, London: Hamish Hamilton-Penguin

MacCannell, Juliet Flower (1991) *The Regime of the Brother: After the Patriarchy*, London and New York: Routledge

McMillan, Peter (1992) *Men, Sex and Other Secrets*, Melbourne: The Text Publishing Company

Mangan, J. A. and James Walvin (eds) (1987) *Manliness and Morality: Middle-Class Masculinity in Britain and America, 1800–1940*, Manchester: Manchester University Press

Marks, Elaine and Isabelle de Courtivron (eds) (1980) *New French Feminisms: An Anthology*, Brighton: Harvester

Metcalf, Andy and Martin Humphries (eds) (1985) *The Sexuality of Men*, London and Sydney: Pluto

Middleton, Peter (1992) *The Inward Gaze: Masculinity and Subjectivity in Modern Culture*, London and New York: Routledge

Miles, Rosalind (1991) *The Rites of Man: Love, Sex and Death in the Making of the Male*, London: Paladin-HarperCollins

Money, John (1988) *Gay, Straight, and In-Between: The Sexology of Erotic Orientation*, New York and Oxford: Oxford University Press

Morgan, David H. J. (1992) *Discovering Men*, London and New York: Routledge

Mort, Frank (1987) *Dangerous Sexualities: Medico-Moral Politics in*

England Since 1830, London and New York: Routledge & Kegan Paul

Nardi, Peter M. (ed.) (1992) *Men's Friendships*, Newbury Park: Sage

Opie, Iona and Peter (eds) (1980) *The Classic Fairy Tales*, London: Paladin-Granada

Painton, Priscilla (1993) 'The Shrinking Ten Percent', *Time* (Australian edition), 26 April, pp. 41–3

Parker, Andrew et al. (eds) (1992) *Nationalisms and Sexualities*, New York and London: Routledge

Patton, Paul and Ross Poole (eds) (1985) *War/Masculinity*, Sydney: Intervention Publications

Pleck, Joseph H. and Jack Sawyer (eds) (1974) *Men and Masculinity*, New York: Prentice Hall

Porter, David (ed.) (1992) *Between Men and Feminism*, London and New York: Routledge

Pronger, Brian (1990) *The Arena of Masculinity: Sports, Homosexuality, and the Meaning of Sex*, New York: St Martin's

Radstone, Susannah (ed.) (1988) *Sweet Dreams: Sexuality, Gender and Popular Fiction*, London: Lawrence & Wishart

Reinisch, June M. and Ruth Beasley (1991) *The Kinsey Institute New Report on Sex: What You Must Know To Be Sexually Literate*, London: Penguin

Rodowick, D. N. (1991) *The Difficulty of Difference: Psychoanalysis, Sexual Difference and Film Theory*, New York and London: Routledge

Roper, Michael and John Tosh (eds) (1991) *Manful Assertions: Masculinities in Britain since 1800*, London and New York: Routledge

Rosenthal, Harold and John Warrack (1972) *Concise Oxford Dictionary of Opera*, London: Oxford University Press

Rubin, Gayle (1975) 'The Traffic in Women: Notes on the "Political Economy" of Sex', in Rayna R. Reiter (ed.) *Towards an Anthropology of Women*, New York and London: Monthly Review Press, pp. 157–210

—— (1993; orig. pub. 1984) 'Thinking Sex: Notes for a Radical Theory of the Politics of Sexuality', in Henry Abelove et al. (eds) *The Lesbian and Gay Studies Reader*, New York and London: Routledge, pp. 3–44

Ruse, Michael (1988) *Homosexuality: A Philosophical Inquiry*, London: Blackwell

Russo, Vito (1987) *The Celluloid Closet: Homosexuality in the Movies*, New York: Harper & Row

Rutherford, Jonathan (1992) *Men's Silences: Predicaments in Masculinity*, London and New York: Routledge

Said, Edward W. (1985; orig. pub. 1978) *Orientalism*, London: Penguin

Saunders, Kay and Raymond Evans (eds) (1992) *Gender Relations in Australia: Domination and Negotiation*, Sydney: Harcourt Brace Jovanovich

Sayers, Dorothy L. (1973; orig. pub. 1923) *Whose Body?*, London: Times Mirror-New English Library

Schwenger, Peter (1984) *Phallic Critiques: Masculinity and Twentieth-Century Literature*, London: Routledge & Kegan Paul

Screen (1992) *The Sexual Subject: A* Screen *Reader in Sexuality*, London and New York: Routledge

Seccombe, Wally (1992) *A Millennium of Family Change: Feudalism to Capitalism in Northwestern Europe*, London and New York: Verso

Sedgwick, Eve Kosofsky (1985) *Between Men: English Literature and Male Homosocial Desire*, New York: Columbia University Press

— (1990) *Epistemology of the Closet*, Berkeley and Los Angeles: University of California Press

Segal, Lynne (1990) *Slow Motion: Changing Masculinities, Changing Men*, London: Virago

— and Mary McIntosh (eds) (1992) *Sex Exposed: Sexuality and the Pornography Debate*, London: Virago

Seidler, Victor J. (1989) *Rediscovering Masculinity: Reason, Language and Sexuality*, London and New York: Routledge

— (1991a) *Recreating Sexual Politics: Men, Feminism and Politics*, London and New York: Routledge

— (ed.) (1991b) *The Achilles Heel Reader: Men, Sexual Politics and Socialism*, London and New York: Routledge

— (ed.) (1992) *Men, Sex and Relationships: Writings from* Achilles Heel, London and New York: Routledge

Showalter, Elaine (1985) *The Female Malady: Women, Madness,*

and English Culture, 1830–1980, New York: Pantheon
— (ed.) (1989) *Speaking of Gender*, New York and London:
    Routledge
Stein, Edward (ed.) (1992) *Forms of Desire: Sexual Orientation and
    the Social Constructionist Controversy*, New York and London:
    Routledge
Stoltenberg, John (1990) *Refusing To Be a Man: Essays on Sex and
    Justice*, New York: Penguin-Meridian
Stone, Lawrence (1979) *The Family, Sex and Marriage in England
    1500–1800*, London: Penguin
Theweleit, Klaus (1987; orig. German pub. 1977) *Male Fantasies,*
    vol. 1, *Women, Floods, Bodies, History*, trans. Stephen Conway,
    with Chris Turner and Erica Carter, Cambridge: Polity
— (1989; orig. German pub. 1978) *Male Fantasies,* vol. 2, *Male
    Bodies: Psychoanalyzing the White Terror*, trans. Chris Turner
    and Erica Carter, with Stephen Conway, Cambridge: Polity
Thompson, Keith (ed.) (1992) *Views from the Male World*, London:
    Aquarian/Thorsons-HarperCollins
Threadgold, Terry and Anne Cranny-Francis (eds) (1990) *Feminine,
    Masculine and Representation*, Sydney: Allen & Unwin
Tolson, Andrew (1977) *The Limits of Masculinity*, London: Tavistock
    Publications
Tulloch, Sara (comp.) (1991) *The Oxford Dictionary of New Words:
    A Popular Guide to Words in the News*, Oxford and New York:
    Oxford University Press
Ujfalussy, József (1971) *Béla Bartók*, trans. Ruth Pataki, rev. Elisabeth
    West, Budapest: Corvina
Vadasz, Danny and Jeffrey Lipp (eds) (1990) *Feeling Our Way: Gay
    Men Talk About Relationships*, Melbourne: Designer Publica-
    tions
Watney, Simon (1987) *Policing Desire: Pornography, AIDS and the
    Media*, London: Comedia-Methuen
Weeks, Jeffrey (1977) *Coming Out: Homosexual Politics in Britain,
    from the Nineteenth Century to the Present*, London: Quartet
— (1985) *Sexuality and Its Discontents: Meanings, Myths, and
    Modern Sexualities*, London: Routledge & Kegan Paul
— (1989) *Sex, Politics and Society: The Regulation of Sexuality since
    1800*, 2nd edn., London and New York: Longman

— (1991) *Against Nature: Essays on History, Sexuality and Identity*, London: Rivers Oram Press

Weinberg, Dr George (1975; orig. pub. 1972) *Society and the Healthy Homosexual*, Gerrards Cross, Bucks: Colin Smythe

Williams, Linda (1990) *Hard Core: Power, Pleasure, and the 'Frenzy of the Visible'*, London: Pandora

Opera and film

Bartók, Béla (1966; orig. composed 1911) *Bluebeard's Castle*, op. 11, libretto by Béla Balázs, trans. Chester Kallman, with Christa Ludwig and Walter Berry, cond. Istvan Kertesz, London Symphony Orchestra, London-Decca, OSA 1158

Pollack, Sydney (dir.) (1982) *Tootsie*, with Dustin Hoffman, Jessica Lange and Terri Garr, Columbia Pictures

Ray, Nicholas (dir.) (1955) *Rebel Without a Cause*, with James Dean, Natalie Wood and Sal Mineo, Warner Brothers

Wilder, Billy (dir.) (1959) *Some Like It Hot*, with Marilyn Monroe, Tony Curtis and Jack Lemmon, MGM

Index

post-traumatic stress disorder, 10; *see also* shell-shock
power, x, 18, 30, 77; and age, 34; and patriarchy, 33–8; and penis, 77–80; and phallus, 77–80; and physical strength, 34; and physique, 34; and sexual difference, 77–80; and sexual orientation, 34; and sexual prowess, 34; images, of, 40; and virility, 44
practice, sexual, 14
practices, social, 7
Prohibition, 66
propaganda, political, 76
Protestant Ethic and the Spirit of Capitalism, The, 27–8

'Race, Sexual Politics and Black Masculinity', x
rape, 43; and judicial ruling, 31; within marriage, 31–2
reading against the grain, 48
Rebel Without a Cause, 72
Red Therapy, 23
Rediscovering Masculinity, 23
religion, and gender, 4
revolution, industrial, 11
revolution, sexual, 11–13; and HIV/AIDS, 13–14
rhetoric, 52; of gender, 52
Rhinegold, the (in *The Ring of the Nibelungs*), xiii
Ring of the Nibelungs, The, xiii
rivalry, male, 36
Rodin, Auguste, 82
roles: male and female, 9; traditional gender, 17
Rosalind (in *As You Like It*), 65
Rosenthal, Harold, 28
Rubin, Gayle, xi, 4
Ruse, Michael, 61

safe-sex campaign, 14; *see also* HIV/AIDS
safe-sex practices, 13–14; *see also* HIV/AIDS
Said, Edward, xi
St Valentine's Day Massacre, 66
Salk Institute, 5

Samber, Robert, 91
Sandy (in *Tootsie*), 49
satyr, the, 80
Sawyer, Jack, 23
Sayers, Dorothy L., 10; *see also Whose Body?*
Schlafly, Phyllis, 62
Screen, 92
Sebastian, Saint, 45
Sedgwick, Eve Kosofsky, 36
Seidler, Victor J., 23
'Self', the, 92
self-referentiality, 52
semen, excess of, 13
semiotics, 4, 51, 53; of gender, 51
sentimentalism, 41
sex: as competitive, 44; binary relation to gender, xi, 3; third, 57–8; *see also* intercourse
sex drive, male, 12–13; *see also* desire
sex/gender system, xi, 4
sexes: differences between, 88; division between, 6
sexism, male, 15
sexual intercourse, *see* intercourse
sexual pleasure: female, 44; male, 44
sexual practice, 14
sexuality, female: and men's understanding, 44
sexuality, male, xii, 12, 13–14, 44; and masturbation, 41, 44; and sexual penetration, 43–5; and the adolescent, 44; as free of responsibility, 13–14; as natural, 13–14; myth of, 13; power encoded in, 44; power encoded in (heterosexual), 44; power encoded in (homosexual), 44
Shakespeare, William, 65
shell-shock, 9–11; as physical, 9–10; as physiological, 9–10; as psychological, 9
Showalter, Elaine, 9
signs: behavioural, 30; clothing as, 50, 52; gestural, 30, 51; of heterosexual masculinity and gay men, 52
Singer, Steve, 90
SNAG, *see* Guy, Sensitive New Age